MOTHMAN
& OTHER
FLYING
MONSTERS

Published by Lisa Hagan Books 2023

www.lisahaganbooks.com

Cover photography Jonathan Borba

Cover and interior layout by Simon Hartshorne

MOTHMAN & OTHER FLYING MONSTERS

NUCLEAR NIGHTMARES & ARMAGEDDON

NICK REDFERN

CONTENTS

THIS BOOK IS DEDICATED
TO SUSAN SHEPPARD

INTRODUCTION

Back in 1975, when I was just ten-years-old, a book was published that became an absolute classic. In fact, it was an epic production of the occult, the paranormal, the cryptoterrestrial and the supernatural. And altogether combined. As for the "leading character" in the book, he had a pair of burning eyes and gargoyle-style wings. You know who we're talking about.

The title remains unforgettable when you've read the book and seen the various, spectacular artwork to back it up. The name: *The Mothman Prophecies*. The author of this production was the late John Alva Keel, the author of a great, adventurous book called *Jadoo*. The book company said of Keel's *Jadoo* that "...From the Upper Nile to the to the lower Ganges and the Roof of the World in Tibet, John Keel traveled in search of Jadoo – the black magic of the Orient – and had some of the most fantastic experiences ever to appear on the printed page."

Wow! Impressive! Even at my early time, I knew I was set for a life like that. There simply was nothing else I could do: it was adventure or zero. Now, back to *The Mothman Prophecies*.

STRANGE THINGS WERE BEGINNING

The book told of the wild, sinister 1966-1967 story of a menacing red-eyed, winged monster that plagued the little city of Point Pleasant, West Virginia. And the word "prophecies" became very apt. It wasn't long before people around the town were having nightmarish dreams of disaster, chaos and even death. And, no less, some of those grim prophecies came to absolute realities.

The flying monster had carefully placed itself in the city – and by both day and night.

DOWN IN THE GRAVEYARD AND THE MAN WHO SMILED LIKE A MANIAC

There's something else very important, too: it has been wrongly assumed that the first encounter with Mothman took place in Point Pleasant. Not at all. The first confrontation – we're told - was on the night of November 12, 1966. The location was a cemetery in Clendenin, which is close to eighty-miles from Point Pleasant.

The grave-diggers, who were on-site at the time, were shocked and awed when they saw what was described as "a brown shape with wings." The creature vanished into the blackness leaving the men shaking. Three days later a group of amazed kids – Roger Scarberry, Linda Scarberry and Steve and Mary Mallette – had their night-time encounter; an encounter that just about defined the legend of Mothman. Deputy Millard Halstead said: "I've known these kids all their lives. They'd never been in any trouble and they were really scared that night. I took them seriously." So did many others, too.

In that period of 1966 and 1967, there was a huge amount of strange activity in the area: Mothman; the pale-faced, Men in Black; poltergeist activity; UFOs; and weird and sinister characters that just might not have been quite human. One of them was a "man" who went by the name of Indrid Cold. A man who was known for his terrible, wild grin. In fact, the Grinning Man of today was clearly born out of Indrid Cold. We'll hear much more about this half-human thing later on.

AN EXPLOSIVE AREA

There used to be an old TNT plant in the area. But, no more. It has pretty much been razed to the ground. Much of the area is empty, abandoned and covered in overgrown bushes, vines and moss, and hidden by the trees. Graffiti adorns the old structures – some with imagery of Mothman himself. The setting – and particularly so at night – is apocalyptic, to say the very least. Indeed, the ruined, run-down area looks like the kind of locale one might expect to see in the likes of *The Walking Dead* on television. And, decades later, the area still oozes a sense of hard-to-describe menace.

Notably, at the same time the events in Point Pleasant, West Virginia were afoot, very similar things were going down in New York – in Huntington, specifically in an area known to the locals as Mount Misery. Like Point Pleasant, the area was, *and still is*, steeped in weirdness. Strange creatures – such as "black panthers," and ghostly black dogs with eyes like burning coals – roam the heart of the old woods. Ghostly children have been seen wandering the old lanes after the sun has set.

NOT THE KIND OF LOVE YOU WOULD WANT

Creepy Men in Black have knocked on the doors of locals late at night, warning them not to discuss the supernatural activity that dominates the area. And, for years, Mount Misery – with its thick, dense canopies of trees – has been a beacon for lovers. We'll come back to the "Lovers Lane" aspect of all this later on, as it played a very important picture in the 1960s…*and still does*.

John Keel reported in his 1975 book, *The Mothman Prophecies*, that a young couple – Richard and Jane – after an evening of *hanging* out, and *making* out, were driving to Richard's home when he suddenly fell sick. He was overcome by weakness and nausea and even briefly passed out at the wheel. Not too good.

Fortunately, because of the tight corners on the small, winding roads, Richard was barely driving at fifteen miles per hour, something which allowed Jane to quickly grab the wheel and bring the car to a screeching halt. The next thing Jane remembered was seeing a bright flash, followed by a groggy sense of missing time and a feeling of memories of…well, *something*.

MORE NEGATIVITY

There is, however, another angle to the history of the area: Point Pleasant, West Virginia is a city of around four-and-a-half-thousand people. In 1774, the city became the site of a now-historic battle between the forces of Colonel Andrew Lewis and Native Americans from the Shawnee and Mingo groups, and overseen by Shawnee Chief Cornstalk. It was a bloody and violent battle that Cornstalk's people lost. Despite the historic nature of the battle, there is no doubt that it has been eclipsed by a series of events which occurred between November 1966 and December 1967: it can only be the reign of Mothman.

DEATH ON TERRIBLE LEVELS

Just before Christmas of 1967, there was death on the Ohio River. Or, rather, I should say there was death *under* the waters. On the evening of December 15, forty-six people drowned when the Silver Bridge – that spanned the Ohio River – collapsed. After the awful disaster, the sightings of Mothman dropped hugely. Since then, there have only been sporadic sightings of Mothman in and around – and in other parts of West Virginia. To this day, there are many who believe the cause of the death and the mayhem was due to Mothman. A real-life grim-reaper gone insane? Perhaps. There's another thing, too: some of those prophecies proved to be true. We'll come to that later on.There is another angle to all off this, too.

SAUCER SMEAR AND THE SILVER BRIDGE

One day, and not long ago, when I was near to finishing the book you're reading right now, I was chatting with a few friends about Gray Barker's Mothman-themed book, *The Silver Bridge* that was published in 1970. Barker was a skilled writer and the first person (in 1956) to write a book on the Men in Black. Its title is *They Knew Too Much About Flying Saucers.* I've come to know over the years that many people don't realize that the first book on the subject of Mothman was *not* John Keel's book. *The Mothman Prophecies* wasn't published until 1975. Barker's book hit the shelves in 1970. I have to say that Barker's writing style was much better than Keel's. It was far more gripping. But, there's a problem....

LYING IN THE SKY?

By that, I mean Barker chose to go *too far* with both his style and his exaggerated content. And, even worse, it was hard to tell what was real and what was made out of Barker's imagination. Indeed, Barker's style reminds me of the King of Gonzo, Hunter S. Thompson.

In fact, for me, Barker's writing *often* came across like that of Hunter S. Thompson: it was great to read, but was it all true? By that, I mean a mix of fact and fiction and that what became known as "Gonzo" writing. But, as good as his writing was, Barker totally screwed himself because of his need to expand fact into something even more. Or, something that was actually of a lesser nature. At times, Barker exaggerated to the level that, while writing, he could have been called a downright liar.

And, Keel wasn't against hanging out with Barker and UFO hoaxer, Jim Moseley of the newsletter, *Saucer Smear*. So, if you're someone who is interested in the early years of the Mothman phenomenon, certainly get your hands on both books: *The Silver Bridge* of 1970 and *The Mothman Prophecies* of 1975. You'll get some good data out of both books. But, just go carefully and filter out the good from the bad as you go along. Because, filtering *was* definitely needed.

HOW MANY OF THESE WINGED MONSTERS ARE THERE?

Now, it's time for *me* to share with *you* my own findings on that red-eyed, flying thing. Or, to be far more accurately, *things*. I have to say there's clearly not just one of those creeps soaring around the skies. That's totally ridiculous. They have been seen all around the world and for centuries. I often wonder why so many people think there's just *a* solitary winged monster of the air causing havoc and death in the skies. Such a scenario is nonsense. As you will soon find out. It's just the names and the places that are different. I could reel off boxes and boxes of titles for these creatures. Some of them are the Houston Batman of Texas; the Owlman of Cornwall, United Kingdom; and the United States'

Batsquatch. They're all dangerous. Deadly, too. And they are all humanoids and with wings.

TERROR TODAY

The red-eyed monster that surfaced at Point Pleasant in the 1960s was intent on killing dozens of people. And, very unfortunately, it worked. Today's Mothman, however, wants to vaporize billions of people on our planet. That, in essence, is the absolute crux of this book. Over the last six years I have come to know that more and more people are having terrifying nightmares in the dead of night. In most of the imagery, it's of nuked cities flattened, and with civilization utterly over. Everywhere. And that's where this story goes: Images of Mothman and nuclear destruction.

Unfortunately, today's Mothman is far more fierce and deadlier than the monster of 1966-1967. It has nothing less than global nuclear war on its warped mind. Later on, you'll see why, precisely. Today, we're in the nuclear age and so is today's Mothman – and the whole thing is getting more and more dangerous by the day. Just look at the television news. I prefer CNN and *not* the other one. Russia, the Ukraine, muscles flexing from China. That is what this modern monster wants. And, there truly is a method in the madness – as you'll be see. Whereas, in the Sixties, forty-six people drowned on the Silver Bridge on December 15, 1967, today Mothman wants our minds filled with images of a Third World War, with gigantic, radioactive clouds in the sky, and with billions dead. Now, let's see the key to this book: how today's Mothman and the nuclear age came together. And still *are* together.

Nick Redfern, 2023

CHAPTER 1:

EYES OF FIRE

There are two important reasons as to why I became fascinated by the phenomenon known as Mothman. (A) was a 1967-era horror-movie when I was a little kid; and (B) was a sinister, and grisly, real-life saga of the latter part of the 1800s. And, it all took place in central England, just a short time from the huge and creepy Cannock Chase woods that still stand today. In a very strange fashion both things had connections to monsters in the sky. As you'll see.

That might sound like a bizarre quest to try and solve an adventurous secret. But, it was much more than that. We'll start with that 1960s-era horror movie that has always been one of my favorites. No, it wasn't one of the classic movies that Hammer Film Productions made so well in the Sixties and that both Christopher Lee and Peter Cushing starred in time and time again. The movie is titled *The Blood Beast Terror*. And it was made in 1967.

Remember that year; it's important. The movie was made by Tigon, and was right up there with Hammer. It would be. Peter Cushing was in that too, even though he was primarily known for his work with Hammer.

Now, back to why the movie caught my attention: set in the 19th century, it tells of a definitive mad scientist who has created

a monster. Not a werewolf. Not a Vampire. Rather, he has created nothing less than...*a giant moth with red eyes.* No, I'm not
joking. How weird is that? In the movie, it's not long before the
beast becomes uncontrollable. Peter Cushing takes on the role of
Inspector Quennell. His team of policemen do their best to save
the locals from violent, bloody deaths. And, of course, there's a hot,
buxom babe on the scene. In this case, her name –in the movie – is
Clare Mallinger. In the real world, her name is Wanda Ventham.
Her son is Benedict Cumberbatch, who played an updated, and
upgraded, Sherlock Holmes for the modern era. The show was
very well received and ran from 2010 to 2017.

FROM FICTION TO FACT – OR IS IT THE OTHER WAY AROUND?

Now, we get to the most important part of the story: the mov-
ie-monster itself. It's a horrific, giant moth with glowing, blazing
eyes. And it comes out at night to feed. Unfortunately, it feeds on
us: people. I won't share anymore of the story with you; but there's
something very important for you to know: *The Blood Beast Terror*
went into the planning mode in 1967. One year later, the movie
was being shown at cinemas in the U.K. I have to say I loved the
movie. That is, when my parents allowed me watch it. I was only
two years old when the movie was filmed and, I can understand
why they didn't want me seeing it at that age! But, when I was four
or five years old, I remember me and my dad watching a rerun
of the movie. It was, without doubt, great! I still watch it to this
day. Now, I have an important question for you:
    Were the uncanny similarities between the blood beast in the
movie, and the appearance of the Mothman at Point Pleasant, just
coincidences? Did someone at Tigon studios hear about what

was going on at Point Pleasant in 1967 and decided to make a movie involving a deadly, man-sized moth with blazing eye-balls? Or, was there some kind of truly bizarre zeitgeist going down in the United Kingdom? Whatever the answers to those questions might be, I can tell you that *The Blood Beast Terror* became one of my favorite movies. In fact, it still is. As a little kid, the image of that giant movie-moth hit me like a bolt. Why? I really don't know. But, there's no doubt something pulled me to the movie time and time again. Now, there's the other part of the story, the part that involved yet *another* flying nightmare of the darkness. Get ready for it.

MAYHEM AND "A LARGE MALICIOUS AVIATOR"

I grew up in a small, picturesque old village in central England. Its title: Pelsall. And when I say "old" I'm not exaggerating. So far as can be determined, Pelsall was built as far back as 994 AD. In 1994, the village folk of Pelsall celebrated their one thousand years of existence. How should I describe Pelsall? Well, if you enjoy those U.K. TV shows, like *Midsomer Murders*, and you enjoy old architecture, you'll love the place. Although I have lived in the United States for twenty-five years, I still get back now and again to that little village I was born in, to hang out with all my old school friends for a few pints of chilled beer. Or, for quite a few.

Pelsall is only a very short drive to a place called Great Wyrley; maybe only a fifteen-minute drive. It, too, is ancient and pictur-esque. Now, to the sinister side of the story. The town was almost turned over with fear when, in 1903, a number of horses in the area were violently killed by...well...you take your guess. The theories, as to who or what was behind the terrible killings of the poor horses were many. Those same theories included a number of giant wild boar, a hypnotized ape (no, I'm *not* joking), and some kind of fierce, powerful, wild cat that had escaped from a private menagerie. Most people, however, put the crime on a young local man named George Edalji, who was jailed for his alleged awful actions in 1903.

As *Making Britain* say: "Edalji was arrested for these crimes and despite an alibi was found guilty and sentenced to seven years in prison. His father worked tirelessly to publicize the case and his son's innocence. Suddenly, in 1906, Edalji was released from prison with no explanation or pardon. He was unable to return to work and therefore sought to clear his name after his release…Suddenly, in 1906, Edalji was released from prison with no explanation or pardon."

Much of the help came from none other than Arthur Conan Doyle, the man who wrote the Sherlock Holmes stories. The fact that George's family came from Bombay, India, suggested that (a) there was a great deal of racial hatred in the area; and (b) George had been set-up, because the townsfolk just didn't like him. To his credit, however, George worked hard and practiced as a lawyer. He had a good, solid life and lived with his sister, Maud, until his death in 1953.

As for those who continued to search for the attacker(s) of the horses, one said, intriguingly, that the culprit was – and I quote – "*a large malicious aviator.*" In other words…a huge, winged beast: "a great bird of prey." I have to say that living in Pelsall - and only a few miles away from Great Wyrley – I heard the story of George Edalji on many occasions as a kid. Often it would be told in the nearby, dense, aged woods, by eager and knowing locals, when snow was coming down and there was plenty of creepy atmosphere.

I really don't know why, but I became fascinated by that huge, winged thing that soared across the skies of Great Wyrley when darkness arrived. And that was just a few miles from where me and my parents lived then. So, those were the two "things" that got me into the Mothman mystery: (A) that elusive, giant "aviator" and (B) the 1968 movie about the giant, deadly moth, *Blood Beast Terror.*

As a kid, I couldn't walk away from either subjects. I don't think I can now. But both things are embedded in my mind. Why? I'm not sure; but strange, flying monsters have been in my mind since I was a little kid. Soon, we'll have an answer, a very bizarre answer. We'll also have another flying monster.

CHAPTER 2:

FROM A MOTHMAN TO AN OWLMAN

This undeniably weird saga that you are about to be exposed to, began in the summer of 1976. I was eleven years old. The location: the old hills and foggy moors of the ancient counties of Cornwall and Devon, England. Of course, there has to be a monster in the story, right? Right! The areas are still peppered with the remains of ancient stone circles. At that time, I was off school for six wonderful weeks: it was the vacations. The locals – and the media, too – quickly heard whispered rumors about a blazing-eyed monster that became known as the Owlman. Yes, I know, it sounds like an awful super-hero. But, it wasn't. Not at all. The Owlman was a violent, almost-man-sized monster with wings and an eerie owl-like face. Mostly, it lurked around the old Mawnan Church. That's where a string of girls – who happened to be in the area and at the right time - were plunged into states of terror when the Owlman attacked them.

FROM CHURCH TO MONSTER AND THEN TO TERROR

As for the history of the monster-plagued church, there's this: "The ancient Church of St. Mawnan is on the headland where the

Helford River meets the sea. It is accessible from the South West Coast Path and attracts many walkers and other visitors. Mawnan is probably named after a sixth century Saint Maunanus. Little is known about him, but probably he was a Breton monk who landed here about 520 AD."

I have to make it clear that I hadn't heard of the original sightings of the Owlman in 1976, even though I was in the area at that time. I was only eleven years old then, and far more interested in punk rock, soccer, horror movies and girls. Those interests continued, but they were also expanded to the domain of monster-hunting. I remember that, around 1980 (when I was fifteen), I wrote a story about the Owlman at my school. I didn't do anything with the story; but, I guess it made me feel like I was a writer. No chance at that age! However, I *did* write an article on the Owlman further down the line. That would have been around 1982, when I was coming up to twenty. And here it is:

In 1976 the dense trees surrounding Mawnan Old Church, Cornwall, England became a magnet for a deadly monster that was christened the Owlman. The majority of those who crossed paths with the creature said it was human-like in both size and design. And possessed a pair of large wings, red eyes, and a lot of menace. No wonder people make parallels with Mothman. It all began during the weekend of Easter 1976, when two young girls, June and Vicky Melling, had an encounter of a truly nightmarish kind in Mawnan Woods. The girls were on holiday with their parents when they saw a gigantic, feathery "bird man" hovering over the 13th Century church.

It was a story their father, Don Melling, angrily shared

with a man named Tony "Doc" Shiels. I say "angrily" because Shiels was a noted, local magician who Melling came to believe had somehow instigated the whole affair. Or as Shiels, himself, worded it: "…some trick that had badly frightened his daughters." Shiels denied any involvement in the matter, whatsoever. But that was only the start of things.

Another one to see the Owlman was Jane Greenwood, also a young girl. She wrote a letter to the local newspaper, the *Falmouth Packet*, during the summer of 1976 that detailed her own startling encounter: "I am on holiday in Cornwall with my sister and our mother. I, too, have seen a big bird-thing. It was Sunday morning, and the place was in the trees near Mawnan Church, above the rocky beach. It was in the trees standing like a full-grown man, but the legs bent backwards like a bird's. It saw us, and quickly jumped up and rose straight up through the trees. How could it rise up like that?"

Two fourteen year old girls, Sally Chapman and Barbara Perry, also had the misfortune to have a run-in with the Owlman in 1976. At around 10.00 p.m., while camping in the woods of Mawnan, and as they sat outside of their tent making a pot of tea, the pair heard a strange hissing noise. On looking around, they saw the infernal Owlman staring in their direction from a distance of about sixty feet.

Sally said: "It was like a big owl with pointed ears, as big as a man. The eyes were red and glowing. At first I thought that it was someone dressed-up, playing a joke, trying to scare us. I laughed at it. We both did. Then it went up in the air and we both screamed. When it went up you could see its feet!"

Barbara added: "It's true. It was horrible, a nasty owl-face with big ears and big red eyes. It was covered in grey feathers. The claws on its feet were black. It just flew up and disappeared in the trees.

THE OWLMAN WAS NOT GONE, THOUGH

While there were rumors of additional sightings of the creature in the immediate years that followed, it wasn't until the 1980s that the Owlman really put in an appearance that can be documented to a significant degree. In this case, the witness was a young boy, dubbed "Gavin" by a good friend of mine, Jon Downes (who wrote an entire book on the winged monster, titled *The Owlman and Others*), and his then-girlfriend, Sally.

The beast, Gavin told Jon, was around five feet in height, had large feet, glowing eyes, and significantly sized wings. It was a shocking, awe-inspiring encounter that Gavin and Sally never forgot. Neither did my same good friend and full-time monster-hunter, Jon Downes – whose obsession for the flying creature ran for years.

There's another strange thing about this particular chapter. When it comes to the Owlman, - and to other winged monsters when people are in the terrifying presences of these dangerous, flying monsters - they find themselves in states of near-endless bad luck and illness. These creatures will crush you down; even kill you if they wish. Remember what happened when Mothman was seen at Point Pleasant, West Virginia from 1966 to 1967? Dozens of people were drowned in the Ohio River.

Jon Downes experienced that very same pulverizing negativity at close level when he chose to investigate the Owlman phenomenon. Jon tried his very best to stop it all, but it didn't work. Here's what Jon had to say about what he calls "psychic backlash." In the 2006 edition of Jon's book, *The Owlman and Others*, he wrote: "I never believed in it." Then, while still working on the Owlman enigma, Jon said: "My pet cats died suddenly, two computers blew up (as did two cars) and my wife left me."

JON WISHED HE DIDN'T GET INVOLVED. I COULDN'T BLAME HIM

Jon's final words on this affair of supernatural negativity: "In the penultimate chapter, I tell the story of how I did my best to diffuse the malign effects by use of humor during the early months of 2000. However, our bad experiences with psychic backlash continued apace throughout the year. Toby, my old dog, and his two feline friends, Isabella and Carruthers, all died suddenly within a month of each other. Despite a string of media appearances and successful books we were dogged with financial and emotional problems and by the end of the year we had definitely had enough."

Jon's last words on all of that chaos: "On New Year's Day, together with two very powerful witches from Yorkshire [England], I took part in a nine-hour-long ritual to break the spell once and for all."

Jon chose to walk away from the whole Owlman controversy. He did the right thing, methinks. There was, however, yet another bizarre and dangerous situation; a situation that mirrored Alfred Hitchcock's movie of 1963, The *Birds*. The sudden presence of the Owlman – in the area - was definitely not the only thing causing chaos. For example, have a look at the headlines of the local newspapers during that time: they all reported on dangerous and wild animal / bird attacks in nearby villages. Here are just a few of the eye-opening headlines on the newspapers:

"*Woman claims cats 'imprison' me in my own home;*" "*Suicide birds: Why did they attack?*" "*Massed Birds Win the Battle of Beach-Road;*" and "*Villagers 'afraid of footpath;*"

There was another mysterious matter, too. And I wasn't at all surprised. In the summer of 1976 a wild, monster sea-serpent, by the name of Morgawr, surfaced repeatedly from the depths. Think of that! The Owlman and a sea serpent, both in the area and both seen in 1976.

A SEA MONSTER ON THE RAMPAGE

In August 2010, an English author, good friend, and seeker of all-things weird - Elizabeth Randall - said to me that according to a sensational feature that appeared in the pages of the British *Daily Mail* newspaper that same month, "...a picture has been circulating on the Internet purporting to show a sea monster that, so far, seems to have eluded identification. It was seen off Saltern Cove, Devon, U.K., and has been dubbed by many as a 'new Nessie.' The image appears to show a greenish-brown, long-necked 'something,' with a reptilian-like head, that was trailing a shoal of fish just 30 yards offshore. According to reports the fish beached themselves just a few seconds later."

Liz pushed on: "The photo was sent to the Marine Conservation Society, who have still to decide exactly what it is. Although theories range from a sea serpent to a salt water crocodile. The lady who took the photograph at first thought that it might be a turtle but the Marine Conservation Society (MCS) says that not only do turtles not chase fish, but the description doesn't fit."

Meanwhile, of this very same affair, Jon Downes said: "Me? I think it is a basking shark; I think that what appears to be its back is its tail, and the 'head' is the tip of its nose, but golly, wouldn't I love to be proved wrong!" Who knows?

Others suggested that nothing more than a turtle was possibly the culprit. Photographs that were taken by one of the witnesses, Gill Pearce, however, clearly demonstrated that the neck of the creature was much too long for it to be that of a regular turtle. Pearce took the photos on July 27, and subsequently reported the details of the encounter to the Marine Conservation Society; a spokesperson for whom, Claire Fischer, told the media:

"Gill Pearce spotted the creature about 20 meters from the bay at Saltern Cove, near Goodrington. It was observed at about 15.30 on 27 July but by the time she had got her camera it had moved further out. She spotted it following a shoal of fish which beached themselves in Saltern Cove. The creature remained in the sea, then went out again and followed the shoal - this indicates it's not a turtle as they only eat jellyfish. We would love to know if other people have seen anything like this in the same area and can help clear up the mystery."

It's possible that what was seen was Morgawr, a sea-serpent-style beast that has been reportedly seen for decades in and around Falmouth Bay, Cornwall, England - which, very notably, is situated only one county away from where this latest incident occurred. Variously described as looking like a giant serpent, a monstrous eel, or even a supposedly extinct plesiosaur, Morgawr was first viewed in September 1975 by two witnesses who claimed to have seen a humped animal with "stumpy horns" and with bristles that ran along the length of its long neck, and which apparently had a conger-eel in its huge mouth.

A whole wave of startling encounters with the creature occurred during the period 1975-76, and such reports continue to surface sporadically from time to time and from this very same location. Did Morgawr take a trip along the coast for a brief vacation and to entertain the nation's media? Maybe so! That's certainly what some of the local press said. The joking aside, however, was quickly gone.

ANOTHER STRANGE BIRD IN THE AREA

There is, however, *yet another* aspect to the Owlman mystery – something that suggests the creature has an incredible life-span. Or, even, perhaps, it's immortal. While spending days in a local library, Jon Downes came across an old newspaper that strongly suggested the Owlman was around as far back as 1926! The newspaper was the *Cornish Echo* and the title of the article was: "*Boys Attacked by Strange Bird: Unpleasant Experience Near Porthtowan.*"

It's clear from the story that what those boys saw was not your average bird. Consider this extract from the newspaper: "While proceeding along a road on Sunday evening, midway between Mount Hawke and Porthtowan, two lads had their attention drawn to something fluttering on top of a mine. The younger boy ascended the burrow to ascertain what it was, and on finding a large bird, apparently dead, proceeded to examine it. The boy was instantly attacked, and ran back to his brother, who just managed to throw his coat over the bird to prevent any injuries being done."

Could the creature just have been a large, normal bird? That's unlikely. The newspaper staff reported that: "*The bird measured six-feet-inches* [italics mine] from tip of the wing to the other, and was 3ft. in length. It had a powerful pointed beak six-inches in length, short legs, full- webbed feet striped with green and yellow, and duck-shaped body."

What might this creature have been? Well, consider this: the distance from Porthtowan to where the Owlman was seen way back in 1976 is only 16.2 miles. I suggest a strong connection between the Owlman and that *very* mysterious bird.

I had a chilly thought that, soon, I would be encountering yet another flying humanoid. I was not wrong.

CHAPTER 3:

"A FACE THAT LOOKED LIKE A CROSS BETWEEN A CROCODILE AND A BAT"

Something very strange happened to me in 1982. It was yet *another* case of zeitgeist and it revolved around monstrous winged creatures. It mirrored the affair of *The Blood Beast Terror* movie. Let's have a look at how *vocabulary.com* explain it: "*Zeitgeist* is a word that comes straight from German — *zeit* means 'time' and *geist* means spirit, and the 'spirit of the time' is what's going on culturally, religiously, or intellectually during a certain period. Think about how something like Woodstock symbolized the 1960s: Woodstock was part of the Zeitgeist of the 1960s. Whatever seems particular to or symbolic of a certain time is likely part of its Zeitgeist."

There was something else, too: Nineteen-eighty-two was when I started work and I managed to get a cool, fun job on a newspaper called *Zero*. A high-fly newspaper, it certainly wasn't, but I did work on the music / bands/ gigs side of the operation for a couple of great years. And, that definitely helped me to get into the writing industry.

THERE MUST BE SOMETHING IN THE AIR

As for that Zeitgeist, well, I couldn't miss a new U.S. movie that had just been released. Its title was *Q: The Winged Serpent*. Roger Ebert said of it: "'*Q*' returns to the basic formula, in which a prehistoric creature terrorizes the city. In this case, the creature is a Quetzalcoatl, a mythical Aztec monster with wings and four claws. It apparently has been brought back into existence in connection with some shady human sacrifices at the Museum of Natural History (although this particular subplot is very muddled). It lives in a nest at the top of the Chrysler Building, lays eggs, and terrorizes helpless New Yorkers, who are not sure if this is a real monster or another crazy circulation stunt by Rupert Murdoch."

In the same way I came to realize that *The Blood Beast Terror* mirrored the Mothman phenomenon, something exploded in 1982. One night, my mates and I strolled off to the local *ABC* cinema to see the aforementioned *Q*. And, guess what happened a few days later? Wait for it: a monstrous, winged creature was seen by more than a few people in the skies of the north of England. Most people who were close enough to see the monster, said it looked eerily like a pterodactyl from millions of years ago! So, what was it flying over the old, dark hills at night in north Yorkshire, England? Let's see.

I wrote up a little story about it, thinking I was *very* important at *Zero*. I was *not*! At all! But, it *was* a great mystery; a mystery that I could circulate around the little villages and the hills. There was no denying that. I looked further and further into this weird story of the "English pterodactyl" and I knew there was a good story awaiting to be fully opened. It was a *damned* good story, as FBI agent Dale Cooper might have said on *Twin Peaks*. I later found out that none other than legendary paranormal expert and writer, Andy Roberts, was on the trail of this bizarre affair. A few years later, I polished up the article and wrote it all up in a journal. I always have a journal / diary with me after a bizarre event takes place. And this was *definitely* bizarre. Here are my words from that weekend of fun and excitement and a search for creatures from ancient times.

Here's how that story of mine went ahead at *Zero*:

Pterodactyls in the Skies? Or was that Mothman on new territory?

Imagine driving, late at night, across the foggy moors of central England and coming across what looks like nothing less than a living, breathing pterodactyl! Think it couldn't happen? It already has. From 1982 to 1983, a wave of sightings of such a creature – presumed extinct for 65 million years - occurred in an area called the Pennines, better known as the "backbone of England" and comprised of rolling hills and mountains.

So far as can be determined, the first encounter occurred at a place with the highly apt name of the Devil's Punchbowl, on September 12, 1982. That was when a man named William Green came forward with an astonishing story of what he encountered at Shipley Glen woods. It was a large, grey colored creature, that flew in 'haphazard' style and which possessed a pair of large, leathery-looking wings. The latter point is notable, since it effectively rules out a significantly sized feathery bird, and does indeed place matters into a pterodactyl category.

Seventy-two hours later, a woman named Jean Schofield had the misfortune to see the immense beast at the West Yorkshire town of Yeadon. That the thing was heading for the Leeds/Bradford Airport provoked fears in Schofield's mind of a catastrophic mid-air collision between a passenger plane and the mighty winged thing.

Perhaps inevitably, the local media soon heard of the sightings and the story was given pride of place in the newspapers of the day. While the theory that a large bird of prey had escaped from a menagerie or zoo satisfied the skeptics, it did not go down well with the witnesses, who were sure that what they had encountered was something straight out of the Jurassic era. Rather notably, the media attention brought forth additional witnesses, including Richard Pollock, who claimed he and his dog had been dive-bombed by the monster, which descended on the pair with alarming speed, 'screaming' as it did so. Pollock hit the ground, protecting his dog as he did so. Given the fact that the creature was practically on top of him, Pollock couldn't fail to get a good look at it: he described it as reptilian, and with a face that looked like a cross between a crocodile and a bat, which is actually not a bad description of a pterodactyl.

There was then somewhat of a lull in reports; but they exploded again in May 1983. There was a sighting at Thackley on May 6, by a witness whose attention to the creature was provoked by the sudden sound of heavy wings beating above. Yet again, it was a case that not only caught the media's attention but provoked others to come forward. One of them was a Mr. Harris, who said that in

November 1977, at Totley, he saw just such a flying monster that soared overheard, growling as it did so. He was adamant that what he saw was a full-blown pterodactyl. Quite naturally, further attempts were made to try and lay the matter to rest, including the amusing – but utterly unproven – theory that the pterodactyl was actually a radio-controlled model! And claims of escaped, exotic birds were once again trotted out, but without a shred of evidence to support them."

THOUGHTS AND FORMS AND FORMS AND THOUGHTS: THAT'S WHEN THINGS ARE CREATED

To begin with, I thought all of this was down to nothing but a wild coincidence. No, it wasn't a coincidence. Later on, and still as a teenager, I would learn about the phenomenon of the Tulpa. And there was the matter of George Edalji and that giant bird/ bat that was often seen just a few miles from my old home and from Edalji's home. All of those bizarre events that came to me were tied to creatures with huge wings– and with humanoid forms. At certain points I felt like a puppet on strings and being used by these things.

The *PSI Encyclopedia* got it right on target: "The term 'thought-form' describes the concept of an entity created directly and exclusively by the mind, whether unconsciously or consciously, which appears to develop a life of its own, as an independent agent in the real world, perceptible to other people. The belief in thoughtforms is the basis of several related concepts: *tulpa* in Tibet, *pooka* in Germanic and Celtic cultures, and *djinn* or *djinn* in Arabic cultures.

It wasn't until I drove up to the north of England - in my old *Ford Capri* car - that at least some of us realized something crazy was going down that night and on those wild, ancient hills. And what had we done? I'll tell you: that collective plan to try and find a *real* pterodactyl (some chance of that!) resulted in the creation of a Tulpa version of a millions-of-years-old winged monster.

CHAPTER 4:

1984: "WASHINGTON, D.C. IS IN RUINS" AND A RED-EYED, WINGED CREATURE PROWLS AROUND

Two years later, and *still* a teenager, I was working at a central England warehouse where my job was to haul boxes around the building on my forklift truck. Life was good. My little town was filled with girls, music, and nights out with my mates down the local pubs. Something else came along, too. It was something monstrous. Mothman or something that was very much of its ilk. I thought to myself: not *another* clash with a flying monster? Could that really happen to me again? Apparently, yes, it *could* happen. And it *did* happen. There's something else, too.

At that time –1984 - in the U.K. there was a great deal of concern about a potential Third World War with the Russians. People were worried. No, let me put myself right: they were *terrified*. And no-one, for sure, could do anything about it. This led me to put together another small news article for printing.

There was something else, too. It wouldn't be very long, at all, before the BBC would be broadcasting a fictional story about nuclear war. Its title was *Threads*. I distributed copies of the home-made article around all of town and stuck them on nearby buildings. The police were not happy with me, at all. Blow them. In fact, they were beyond angry. Neither was the manager of the company I worked for. The rest of my friends at work *did* like it, but it worried them. That was the point, though.

Now…believe it or not, the article led me *directly* to a… *Mothman-type entity*. I know it sounds over the top, but it's one hundred percent honest. Here's my article:

No-one can win a world war, everyone knows that

Anyone who thinks that riding out a nuclear attack is possible is sadly deluding themselves. Complete and utter chaos, overwhelming destruction, terror, fear, hysteria and - most of all - death on scales almost unimaginable - on both sides - will be the order of the day. And for the next few hundred years. Society will quickly collapse and the "every man for himself" approach will become the rule of law. Lives will be cut short as a result of the radiation. Malnutrition and illness will take more. Many will likely take their own lives. The fact is that no nuclear-armed nation on the planet can launch its missiles without the other side knowing - and responding - in quick-time. And, their missiles will be high in the skies before ours even arrive (and vice-versa). So, for anyone who thinks that kicking the ass of the other side is going to be a breeze, then wise-up. No one will win. No-one can win. Most of us will die. Civilization, as we know it, will not recover. In its place will be a grim world filled with irradiated people, probably in states of mental collapse, and barely able to operate.

Nuclear war has been portrayed in many memorable productions, including *Dr. Strangelove*, *The Day After*, and a 1960s-era show of the BBC, *The War Game* - which was banned from being broadcast not just for years but for decades. *The Day After* gave its viewers at least some hope that life will go on and the human race will overcome the apocalypse. *Threads* will give them no hope. Instead, *Threads* will give the viewers just about the worst possible scenario: a world in ruins and billions dead. In other words, *Threads,* will certainly show the truth. And people need the truth.

Last week, over a couple of beers, I was chatting with a few friends whose political views are very different to mine. Put it this way: I'm a labor guy [that means a Democrat]. They're not. But, it doesn't stop us all from hanging out and having a good time. One of the things that surprised me, though, as we knocked back the beer, was their approach to the matter of nuclear war. There can hardly be anyone out there who hasn't heard all of the recent statements, concerns, and worries of a nuclear Armageddon and a looming Third World War. The United States, Russia - everyone is on edge. As we hung out in the bar, I suggested that if the unthinkable should happen it will be the end of civilization - and by that I pretty much meant everywhere. I was, then, amazed, when a couple of my friends said, words to the effect of, 'We can beat them all, hands down.'

You too may have seen this growing and disturbing assumption/trend that, somehow, a nuclear war - involving the major powers of this planet - can somehow be won.

Let's be clear on the matter: no-one can win a nuclear war. Period. Hiding in the bathroom, or under the bed, will do you absolutely no good at all when a city-obliterating nuke detonates within a few miles of you. And, if you are 'lucky' enough to survive the thousands of nukes that are raining down all across the landscape, there's the matter of deadly radiation to deal with too. Add to that, starvation, gangs of people desperate for food and who will kill to get what they need to survive, and rampant disease and no fresh water, and the picture is hardly a positive one.

Anyone who thinks that riding out a nuclear attack is possible is sadly deluding themselves. Complete and utter chaos, overwhelming destruction, terror, fear, hysteria and - most of all - death on scales almost unimaginable - on both sides - will be the order of the day. And for the next few hundred years. Society will quickly collapse and the 'every man for himself' approach will become the rule of law. Lives will be cut short as a result of the radiation. Malnutrition and illness will take more. Many will likely take their own lives.

The fact is that no nuclear-armed nation on the planet can launch its missiles without the other side knowing - and responding - in quick-time. And, their missiles will be high in the skies before ours even arrive (and vice-versa). So, for anyone who thinks that kicking the ass of the other side is going to be a breeze, you should wise-up. No-one will win. Most of us will die. Civilization, as we know it, will not recover. In its place will be a grim world filled with irradiated people, probably in states of mental collapse, and barely able to operate.

THE BBC SUCCESSFULLY TERRIFIES
MOST OF THE U.K. IN AN HOUR

Those were the last words of my article. And in the days leading up to the BBC broadcast, the show was highlighted significantly. Everyone I knew was going to settle in, sit down, and watch it. And they did. And I think just about everyone had a sleepless night afterwards, realizing what nuclear war would *really* be like. I remember there was nothing but talk of *Threads* for the next few days at the warehouse. Just about everyone was asking the same question: "Did you see *Threads*?" The others at work were not just quiet, but *beyond* quiet, if there's such a thing.

That, however, was just the start of things. And, guess what? Not long after the jolt that *Threads* made, a red-eyed, winged monster surfaced; albeit in a very weird way. And it all involved none other than *Communion* writer Whitley Strieber. Threads and connections were everywhere.

WARDAY: ANOTHER NUCLEAR NIGHTMARE

Nineteen-eighty-four was the year in which Whitley Strieber penned a nightmarish politics-war story about a nuclear confrontation between the Russians and the United States, and with other nations dragged in. His novel was titled *Warday*. It was written with James Kunetka. I didn't know too much about Strieber at that point in time, apart from having read his earlier book of 1978, *The Wolfen*, which was a great book. Strieber's alien abduction-driven book, *Communion*, of 1987, really made me look more at his work when *Warday* was released. It became a huge bestseller. But, there was something else, too. Something both unsettling and amazing.

The story of *Warday* is both disturbing and engrossing. Thankfully, the super-powers do not erupt into a full-scale, worldwide, nuclear war. But, even on a limited scale, the United States is left in a state of chaos with around twenty percent of the American population killed, and even more dying from the effects of blasts, burns, starvation, disease, and radiation poisoning. It's also very well worth to note what Strieber wrote in his apocalyptic story. At one point, one of the characters says:

"*There is a gigantic beast with bat wings and red, burning eyes that has attacked adults and carried off children. The creature stands seven feet tall and makes a soft whistling noise. It is often seen on roofs in populated areas, but only at night.* [Italics mine]"

Strieber further writes: "*I had just gotten off the Glendale trolley when I heard this soft sort of cooing noise coming from the roof of a house. The sound was repeated and I turned to look toward the house. Standing on the roof was what looked like a man wrapped in a cloak. Then it spread its wings and whoosh! it was right on top of me.* [Italics mine]."

Later on, I made some notes when I saw those words about Strieber's red-eyed, winged monster. After all, Strieber was practically describing Mothman – and there was a "nuclear war" connection, too. I still have those wrinkly notes. Then, when the 1990s came around, I was able to expand the Strieber-Mothman links and leads:

It's important to note – in light of the Mothman-like references – that *Warday* is not a piece of wild science-fiction.

The story of the winged monster is only included in the book to demonstrate how, in the aftermath of the war, strange and bizarre rumors surface and spread among the survivors. I did, however, find it fascinating that *Warday* makes a connection between a nuclear war and a gigantic beast with bat wings and red, burning eyes. This is, of course, what is now being reported today: flying humanoids and nightmares of Mothman. And, let's not forget that Strieber is an alien abductee; one of the most famous and visible ones of all.

Rather notably, back in 1995, Strieber, himself, had a terrible nightmare of a nuclear explosion that destroys Washington, D.C. in the year of 2036 – something that sees the end of the U.S. government as we know it today and the rise, in the wake of the disaster, of a full-blown dictatorship. In his 1997 book, *The Secret School*, Strieber says of this dream (or of a brief view of what is to come via a future self) that: "…Washington, D.C. is in ruins. However, this isn't the center of the memory. The center of the memory is that it was suddenly and completely destroyed by an atomic bomb, and nobody knows who detonated it."

All of this leads us to another nuclear nightmare and another flying creature. The location this time? I'll tell you: the Chernobyl Nuclear Power Plant, constructed not far from the city of Pripyat in the north of the Ukrainian SSR in the then-Soviet Union. On April 26, 1986, disaster did its very worst.

Now, we go to London.

CHAPTER 5:

BEWARE OF THE BRENTFORD GRIFFIN

Although I wasn't able to get involved in this particular "winged-thing" story of 1985, I was, certainly able to put together a coherent view of what went down. And, I can tell you, *a hell of a lot* went down. A dangerous, flying beast thing seen over London, England? That's *exactly* what happened. I'll share with you the full story. With that said, let's take a look at what are now crumpled old notes of mine from the eighties:

Was a centuries-old creature hovering over the U.K.?

"Stories of so-called griffins date back millennia, to the times of the ancient Greeks, Egyptians, and Persians. In the 14th century, Sir John Mandeville wrote of griffins:

"Some men say that they have the body upward as an eagle and beneath as a lion; and truly they say sooth that they be of that shape. But one griffin hath the body more great and is more strong than eight lions, of such lions as be on this half, and more great and stronger than an hundred eagles such as we have amongst us.

"For one griffin there will bear, flying to his nest, a

great horse, if he may find him at the point, or two oxen yoked together as they go at the plough. For he hath his talons so long and so large and great upon his feet, as though they were horns of great oxen or of bugles or of kind, so that men make cups of them to drink of. And of their ribs and of the pens of their wings, men make bows, full strong, to shoot with arrows and quarrels.

"Almost a year later after his extraordinary encounter with a winged creature in the skies over Brentford, London, specifically in February 1985, one Kevin Chippendale saw the flying monster yet again. Others saw the monster, too. They included a psychologist named John Olsen – who encountered the beast while jogging near the River Thames - and a woman named Angela Keyhoe, who saw the griffin squatting in ominous and beady-eyed fashion atop the town's Waterman Carts Center.

"Both the local and national media – television and newspapers – were soon onto the story, and major coverage was afforded the mystery. Then, like so many cryptid-based incidents, the weird wave of the winged thing came to a sudden end. It's worth noting, however, that despite the incredible nature of the affair, this is far from being the only occasion upon which a griffin has been encountered in the UK. There is, however, a long history of Griffins:

"Elliott O'Donnell was an enthusiastic collector and disseminator of data on all manner of wonders, including ghosts, demons, and strange creatures. He was also someone who crossed paths with the English griffin. He said, of a strange story that dated back to the 17th century: 'Mr. John Luck, a farmer from Raveley, set out on horseback one morning to the annual fair at Whittlesea. On the way he met a friend, with whom he had a drink at a wayside inn. After drinking somewhat heavily Mr. Luck became very merry, and perceiving that his friend was getting restless and desirous of continuing on his way to the fair, he said, 'Let the devil take him who goeth out of this house today.'

"The more he drank, the merrier he grew. Forgetful of his rash saying, he called for his horse and set out for the fair. The fresh air seemed to have a sobering effect, for he had not travelled very far before he remembered what he had said. He was naturally superstitious and became so perturbed that he lost his bearings. He was endeavoring to find the way home – it was getting dusk and far too late to go to the fair – when he espied 'two grim creatures before him in the likeness of griffins.

"They handled him roughly, took him up in the air, stripped him, and then dropped him, a sad spectacle, all gory, in a farm yard just outside the town of Doddington. There he was found lying upon some harrows. He was picked up and carried to a house, which belonged to a neighboring gentleman. When he had recovered sufficiently to talk, he related what had happened to him. Before long he 'grew into a frenzy,' so desperate that the inmates of the house were afraid to stay in the room with him.

"Convinced that Luck was under evil influences, they sent for the clergyman of the town. No sooner had the clergyman entered the house than Luck, howling like a demon, rushed at him and would have torn him to pieces, had not the servants of the house come to his rescue. They succeeded with great difficulty in overcoming Luck and tying him to the bed. No one was allowed to enter his room, the door of which was locked.

"Neil Arnold - a good friend of mine - who has carefully studied the affair of the Brentford Griffin, notes the following: 'O' Donnell goes on to describe how Mr. Luck, the next morning, was found dead in his bed. His body a crooked, broken mess, black with bruises, neck snapped, and tongue hanging from his chasm of a mouth. His face an expression of utmost dread. Many believed that the griffin monsters were sent by Satan and had succeeded in their quest.'"

I have a few words for you if you ever see a Griffin: beware of the beast in the skies. Now, it's time to take a look at the terrible Chernobyl nuclear power station disaster of 1986. In a *very* odd way, *it too*, has a connection to Mothman.

CHAPTER 6:

CHERNOBYL, POWERPLANTS, RUSSIA AND MOTHMAN

As the United States Nuclear Regulatory Commission (NRC) said of the Chernobyl disaster, there was a "...sudden surge of power during a reactor systems test destroyed Unit 4 of the nuclear power station at Chernobyl, Ukraine, in the former Soviet Union. The accident and the fire that followed released massive amounts of radioactive material into the environment."

The U.S. NRC expanded on all of this:

Emergency crews responding to the accident used helicopters to pour sand and boron on the reactor debris. The sand was to stop the fire and additional releases of radioactive material; the boron was to prevent additional nuclear reactions. A few weeks after the accident, the crews completely covered the damaged unit in a temporary concrete structure, called the 'sarcophagus,' to limit further release of radioactive material.

The Soviet government also cut down and buried about a square mile of pine forest near the plant to reduce radioactive contamination at and near the site. Chernobyl's three other reactors were subsequently restarted but all eventually shut down for good, with the last reactor closing in December 2000. The Soviet nuclear power authorities presented their initial accident report to an International Atomic Energy Agency meeting in Vienna, Austria, in August 1986.

After the accident, officials closed off the area within 30 kilometers (18 miles) of the plant, except for persons with official business at the plant and those people evaluating and dealing with the consequences of the accident and operating the undamaged reactors. The Soviet (and later on, Russian) government evacuated about 115,000 people from the most heavily contaminated areas in 1986, and another 220,000 people in subsequent years.

Grim? It was beyond grim

Most bleak of all was this from the NRC: "The Chernobyl accident's severe radiation effects killed 28 of the site's 600 workers in the first four months after the event. Another 106 workers received high enough doses to cause acute radiation sickness. Two workers died within hours of the reactor explosion from non-radiological causes. Another 200,000 cleanup workers in 1986 and 1987 received doses of between 1 and 100 rem (The average annual radiation dose for a U.S. citizen is about .6 rem). Chernobyl cleanup activities eventually required about 600,000 workers, although only a small fraction of these workers were exposed to elevated levels of radiation. Government agencies continue to monitor cleanup and recovery workers' health."

The scars – in just about every sense – remain.

NOW, MOTHMAN COMES INTO THE STORY; SURELY, THAT CAN'T BE A GOOD THING?

Now, for the next part of the story, we need to take a look at the 2002 movie version of John Keel's book, *The Mothman Prophecies*. Long-time cryptozoologist, Loren Coleman, was having nothing to do with the quasi-weirdness in the dark skies. Loren said: "*The Chernobyl story, the Galveston Hurricane-Mothman tie-in, and other examples given in the 2002 movie were pure fiction* [italics mine]." That might not actually be the case, though. Or, it might be a bit of the stories stretched in various ways.

After the movie was released, various websites posted that Mothman was the cause of the disaster. Loren continued: "But there is not one thread of evidence that any winged weirdies were witnessed before the Chernobyl accident. It is a bit of movie fiction that has, unfortunately, moved into pseudo-factoid cryptozoology."

THERE STILL COULD BE SOMETHING ELSE, TOO... SOMETHING WE'VE ALL OVERLOOKED...

When I looked into the Chernobyl-Mothman controversy, I decided to look deeper and darker into the rabbit's hole. And, guess what I found? I'll tell you: I unearthed some undeniably interesting things that most definitely had to be revealed. Loren wasn't wrong; not at all. It's just there's more to reveal, as you'll see.

THE MYSTERY BECAME LESS MYSTERIOUS, BUT MORE FASCINATING, TOO

The *Portalist* said: "Reportedly, a bizarre winged creature was seen flying over the town of Chernobyl on numerous occasions. A few workers at Chernobyl also allegedly saw the same creature hovering over the plant. Even stranger, those who claimed to have seen the creature were reportedly plagued by nightmares and harassed by incessant, threatening phone calls thereafter. Many claimed the creature resembled a man-like bird with red eyes, and some came to refer to it as 'the Black Bird of Chernobyl.'"

That was quite a story. The next one is, too.

A PIECE OF ILLUMINATION

I found something that was very intriguing and that was linked to Mothman, Russia, power-plants and John Keel – and all as far as back as 1991. In that year, IllumiNet Press published a then-brand-new edition of *The Mothman Prophecies*. You might not know this, but the 1991 version of Keel's book is slightly different to the other, earlier editions. And, just about ten years later – when the movie version of *The Mothman Prophecies* hit the cinemas - the Afterword proved crucial to how and why the Chernobyl-Mothman affair came to life. Now, we get to the next part of this twisting and twirling story.

A MONSTER OF THE RUSSIAN TYPE

Keel wrote this for IllumiNet: "History does repeat itself and in the 1980s the Soviet Union was suddenly engulfed with stories *and monsters* [italics mine] in a classic repetition of what happened in the USA in the 1950s and 1960s. As in the Great American Wave of those decades, it all seemed to have very important meanings and the innumerable events were subject to all kinds of interpretations ranging from the occult and religious to the scientific and the cosmic. *Bright lights were haunting Soviet atomic plants* [italics mine] and hundreds of remote little Russian towns were plunged into the same kind of *Twilight Zone* horror that once gripped Point Pleasant."

THE CHERNOBYL CONNECTION DOESN'T GO AWAY

Take a closer look at the IllumiNet Press version of *The Mothman Prophecies*. In the Afterword to the book, Keel made *specific* references - *way back in 1991, no less* - to (A) the Soviet Union being *"engulfed with UFOs and monsters;"* (B) *"Soviet atomic plants;"* and (C) *"little Russian towns"* being *"plunged into the same kind"* of horror that descended on Point Pleasant all those years ago.

It's possible that it was Keel, himself, who inadvertently helped to provoke the Chernobyl / Mothman legends. After all, Keel was speaking of such things as far back to the eighties and the nineties. For many, it's incredible to see how Keel's references, in 1991, to Russian atomic facilities, to little Russian towns, and to monsters in Russia – and all in the same breath, no less - could have provoked, such chaos, and provoked bizarre rumors of a looming Chernobyl-type disaster in later years.

That's to say, Keel's Russian-driven words of 1991 could have been provoked – roughly a decade later - by a collective psyche that led to the creation of Tulpa-style thought-forms of Mothman. And, on top of that, when the movie version of *The Mothman Prophecies* was released at cinemas in 2002, things exploded. Mothman was everywhere for a while. People were everywhere. In that sense, Tulpas – of the red-eyed and black-winged type - *really can* manifest. They can be seen. They have life. They can mimic. Possibly, even, at Chernobyl. Keel's very own, deep, long-lasting thoughts of Russian plants, of Russian atomic energy, and of strange creatures in 1991 –in Russia - led life to appear and to remain.

It's clear that Keel, himself, deliberately created those legends back in 1991 to see how far he could go when it came to creating Tulpas. But, Keel didn't know it. Or, possibly, he preferred not to reveal that he, himself, might have played a leading role in creating a bizarre form of life that got out of control. In the skies of Russia.

Now, at this point, Mothman, nuclear technology and night-mares are all beginning to fuse together. The worst is coming.

CHAPTER 7:

PUERTO RICO AND A FIERCE FLIER IN THE AIR

It was 2004 when my good friend and monster-seeker, Jon Downes, and I headed out to the wonderful world of Puerto Rico. A great place. We were there to find a Chupacabra or too. Or, possibly even more. What did we find? That was a good question. We had been hired by the SyFy Channel's show *Proof Positive*. The huge, jungle-like areas are incredible. The hills are huge. Dark, winding caves, and tunnels can be found – if you looked carefully. The streets are peppered with little restaurants and the home-cooked food is amazing. Now, let's get to my notes on this particular road-trip:

An island of unknown flying things

There comes a time in the life of every investigator of the paranormal when a case just gels. From the credibility of the witness to the importance of the story, everything combines together and in the best fashion possible. I have experienced such a deep sense of satisfaction and connection on a number of occasions. But, there is, perhaps, no greater example than the amazing affair of a woman named Norka, which came our way on the fourth day of our beastly trek. Norka was a fascinating lady, who lived in a spacious and atmospheric house high in the El Yunque rain forest. Norka's story was one that took our quest for the truth about the chupacabra to a whole new – and largely unanticipated – level.

After we devoured our breakfasts fit for a king – in the open courtyard of the *Wind Chimes Inn* - our convoy of jeep, cars, and trucks once again hit the road. There were people to interview, creatures to be sought, and absolutely no time to waste. Around ninety minutes after we left bustling San Juan behind us, we arrived at Norka's lavish home. It was dominated by a pair of huge, wrought-iron gates and a driveway that was so steep it actually required me to put the jeep in the lowest possible gear to successfully climb it. I quipped to Jon that the fortified home had probably been built to keep the chupacabra out. Who knows? After digesting what Norka said, I seriously had to wonder if my joke just may have been on target, after all.

Norka, seventy-something and sporting a beaming smile, invited us in as if we were old friends. It almost felt like we were. Norka was an incredibly generous host, despite unfortunately being in failing health. She provided us with liquid refreshment and snacks, gave us a tour of her home - which was, essentially, built solidly into the hill on which it stood - and regaled us with entertaining stories of her youth, during which she was a prize-winning, passionate motorcyclist. Both Jon and I instantly bonded

54

with Norka, who was a fellow adventurer and lover of life – and a highly skilled artist, too.

Roughly an hour after arriving, the crew had set up all of their equipment, the cameras were ready to roll, and me, Jon, and Norka assumed our required positions on the balcony of Norka's home. It provided an incredible, panoramic view of El Yunque. Indeed, the angle of the miles-wide view, coupled with the sheer altitude of Norka's home, provoked a slight sense of vertigo. But that was no matter. Jon and I suspected that Norka had something special to say and we wanted to hear it. We weren't entirely sure *how* special, but we quickly found out.

Norka's words demonstrated that the chupacabra enigma was much older than many researchers had assumed or concluded. Norka's account, we were fascinated to learn, dated from 1975, at the height of the summer months.

The defining event itself was actually the culmination of a series of disturbing attacks on domestic animals in the area in which Norka lived. Tragically, this included an assault on one of Norka's pet dogs, which was found dead, outside the perimeter of her hillside home. It was also found lacking each and every one of its bones, including its skull, no less. How the bones had been savagely removed was something that not even local veterinarians were able to explain. Other families in the area reported their dogs missing, too. They, also, were left with nothing but tears, anguish, presumed dead pets, and a mountain of unanswered questions. As circumstances would have it, and only a couple of weeks later, Norka had an encounter of a kind that would have made horror-maestro H.P. Lovecraft nod approvingly.

It was dusk, on a stiflingly hot, weekday night in August 1975. The atmosphere – as day began to surrender to nightfall – was as normal and tranquil as it had ever been. It wasn't long, however, before normality and tranquility gave way to something hideous. As Norka drove carefully and slowly along the twisting, climbing road (in a car, rather than on one of her trusty motorbikes, I should stress), something suddenly surfaced from the huge, dense trees that stood proud and tall, like gigantic green curtains, and which dominated each side of the road.

Doing barely twenty miles an hour to begin with, Norka was easily able to slow down as a curious beast loomed into view. Norka, looking into the camera, said that only about twenty feet in front of her was the strangest, most terrifying animal it had ever been her misfortune to encounter. For all intents and purposes, it looked very much like a bat. Except, that is, for one astonishing thing: the abomination was around four to five feet in height.

Not surprisingly, Norka could scarcely believe her eyes as the monster shuffled slowly across the road, its muscular legs taking slow but deliberate strides across the hot tarmac. With her eyes transfixed on the beast, Norka could see that its body was dark brown in color. Two large wings were folded tight against its back. The clawed fingers on its hands – that drooped in curious, limp fashion from its bony wrists - were of a distinct, white-yellow hue. Of a near-identical color were two enormous fangs that protruded from its gaping, almost slack-jawed, mouth. Most frightening of all to Norka were the eyes of the creature: focused intently on Norka herself, they were almost blazing, like red hot coals.

After what seemed like a torturous amount of time, but which was maybe no more than twenty or so seconds, the creature unfurled its wings. At this point, Norka could see just how big those mighty, membranous appendages were: somewhere in a combined region of twelve to fifteen feet. Norka said the wings flapped in a fast, furious and loud fashion that deeply shocked her. In mere moments, the beast took to the skies, vertically, and was quickly lost from sight. It was, I said to Jon later, almost a case of the Jeepers Creepers movies come to life. He didn't disagree in the slightest.

Since this was the only interview planned for that day, there was no need for us to make a hasty drive to destinations new, and so we hung out for another hour or so, chatting further with Norka, even though the cameras had stopped rolling. Jon and I were suitably impressed. Our quest for the truth of the chupacabra had taken a major step forward – and, in terms of the date of Norka's encounter, a major step backwards! And there was one more thing:

Norka had so enjoyed the afternoon that she surprised me by presenting me with nothing less than a full-color painting she had created of the creature she encountered back in 1975. I thanked Norka for her incredible generosity. Atmospheric and captivating, her artwork has pride of place on the one and only wall of my office that is not dominated by mountains of bookshelves. *Guess what? The creature that Norka painted had a pair of bright red eyes and large, bat-like wings. Sounds familiar?"* [Italics mine]. There was, however, something else weird on Puerto Rico: a *second* type of winged creature. It was known as the Moca Vampire. Here's how my story went:

Since 1995, Puerto Rico has been the domain of a deadly, bloodsucking creature that has infamously become known as the Chupacabra. Long before the now-legendary beast was on anyone's radar, however, there was another vampire-like monster roaming around on the island. It was known as the Moca Vampire – its name taken from the municipality of Moca, which can be found in the northwest of the island, and which is home to around 40,000 people. Unlike the Chupacabra – sightings of which continue to this very day – the "Vampiro de Moca," as it was referred to on Puerto Rico - was a monster of a definitively "here one minute and gone the next" kind.

The controversy all began in late February 1975. That was when the population of Moca was plunged into a collective state of fear. And it was hardly surprising. Numerous ranchers reported how their farm animals were being violently slaughtered under cover of darkness and systematically drained of massive amounts of blood. The first area targeted was the Barrio Rocha region, where several goats, at least four pigs, numerous chickens, and more than a dozen cows, were all found dead, with puncture marks on their bodies, and deep claw-like wounds on their skin, and all missing one vital ingredient: blood. Villagers and farmers were as outraged as they were terrified. Local authorities, and chiefly the police, tried to diffuse the controversy by attributing the attacks to nothing stranger than the work of packs of wild dogs – a theory that, almost inevitably, was received with nothing but scorn, skepticism, and disdain.

By the end of the first week in March 1975, the death count was close to three dozen. It was in this same week that an important development was made: the blood-sucking culprit was finally seen, up close and personal, so to speak. The witness was a woman named Maria Acevedo, who caught sight a monstrously-sized, screaming and screeching winged beast that landed atop her home, and which clambered about her zinc roof, making an almighty racket in the process. And it was clearly no normal bird: around four to five feet in height, it was described as being similar in appearance to a pterodactyl, a presumed-extinct, flying reptile of the Jurassic era. Whatever the true nature of the monster, it quickly took to the skies and vanished into the starry darkness.

Less than forty-eight hours later, a farmer named Cecilio Hernandez contacted the police after more than thirty of his chickens were killed in a fashion that was quickly becoming attributed to the predations of the Moca Vampire. It was at the same time that Hernandez' story was widely being reported on Puerto Rico that a potential answer to the puzzle was uncovered: two huge snakes were killed in Moca, just before they were about to attack a cow belonging to a rancher named Luis Torres. Of course, this didn't explain the winged monster that Maria Acevedo reported only days earlier. And, it didn't resolve the many and varied additional killings that continued to plague the people of Moca. In addition, while snakes will typically take down and devour – whole, no less - significantly-sized animals, they will not, and cannot, suck blood in either small or large proportions. In other words, while the snake theory might have been a small component of the saga, it most certainly didn't explain everything.

On March 18, 1975, the monster struck again. On this occasion, the victims were a pair of goats owned by Hector Vega, of Moca's Barrio Pueblo. Once again, the culprit had struck in its typical fashion of draining the goats of their blood – and, in this case, of *all* the blood. The creature was not done with Vega, however. On the following night no less than seventeen animals were attacked, of which ten were killed, due to deep, penetrating wounds, trauma, and massive blood loss. Five days later, a pig was found dead by farmer Felix Badillo. Blood was removed in significant amounts, and there was a hole in the head of the animal, which gave every appearance of something powerful being violently thrust into the skull. On top of that, one of the pig's ears was missing – in a fashion that, rather intriguingly, was attributed to a surgical procedure. No wonder the people of Moca were as puzzled as they were alarmed.

Forty-eight hours later came the most astonishing development: Juan Muniz was attacked by a huge, bird-like animal that swopped down upon him from above, as he walked through Barrio Pulido. He struggled and fought as the winged nightmare did its very best to force Muniz to the ground. In his panicked, adrenalized state, Muniz managed to escape and alert the authorities.

Then, as April began, the Moca Vampire began to expand its hunting ground: attacks began to be reported all across the island, with farm animals again drained of blood, of rumors of attacks on people, and even of a police cover-up of the facts to prevent a public panic exploding. The attacks continued into May – and then into June, too. By this time, hundreds of animals were said to have fallen victim to the blood-drinking monster, and with barely an answer to the problem in sight. As it transpired, however, matters came to a sudden, inexplicable halt. Shortly before the end of June, the sightings, encounters and attacks were no more.

Whatever the true nature of the Moca Vampire, it vanished as quickly as it originally surfaced. Such was the terror provoked, however, the creature is still talked about, in hushed tones, in Moca to this very day. The story is *still not* ended, though. When I took a trip to Puerto Rico one year later - 2005 – I found there was another flying thing in the skies of Puerto Rico. This one was a huge, gray, feathery bird that had wings around nine-feet long – on each side. Certainly, this wasn't a Chupacabra or a Moca Vampire. Amazingly, one of the locals in San Juan – the capital city of Puerto Rico – said that, *yes* there *were* several types of flying creatures in Puerto Rico and they spent most of their time in the El Yunque rain-forest, gliding in the darkness. But, for me, the creature that Norka saw was, without doubt, something connected to Mothman. There was no doubt about it.

CHAPTER 8:

"SUSAN, YOU WILL BE MISSED"

This part of the saga is particularly important because the person who told the stories was an incredible person; an expert in the domain of Mothman. She didn't just open-up amazing revelations from the 1960s, when Mothman was at his height. Rather, she uncovered a number of modern-day winged cases, and a handful of strange characters. One of those characters was Indrid Cold; one of the key figures in the Mothman story. He's coming soon.

It was August 28, 2017 and the Mothman Festival was bustling with atmosphere, food, music, and fun. The very first person who I bumped into (and I *do* mean that, literally!) was Susan Sheppard. Susan was both a novelist and an excellent expert on the history of Mothman and the surrounding areas. Indeed, I had seen her speaking on a DVD - *Eyes of the Mothman*- several times.

The words on the back-cover of Susan's book, *The Gallows Tree: A Mothman's Tale*, say: "Author Susan Sheppard grew up only hills away from the first sighting of the West Virginia Mothman that occurred on November 14, 1966. This spectacular event helped shape Sheppard's imagination and set the tone for her future writings."

The back-cover continues on: "Between 1966 and 1967, one hundred sightings of the Mothman were reported by local media.

By 1968, the Mothman had disappeared. But his story did not end there. *In The Gallows Tree: A Mothman's Tale*, the peaceful landscape of West Virginia is shattered by a being that can only be described as a part-human, part-ghoul - a red-eyed, winged beast. Sheppard re-imagines her tale and builds a world for her Mothman through a cast of characters that includes an alcoholic preacher, ghosts of lynched slaves and a beautiful witch queen ruling over local ghouls. In this book, mixed with a dreamlike setting, the Mothman not only comes to West Virginia, he finds his humanity in one stunning final victory."

You really should read it. I have!

FRIENDS WERE MADE, BUT SADLY NOT FOR LONG

There was, however, something else. On that Saturday afternoon at the festival, I got to hang out with Susan for about forty minutes. It was a hot, steaming day and we chatted at my book-table and got into matters relative to one of the creepiest characters in Mothman history. I'm sure you know the one I'm talking about. It was the man with the slightly Dickensian-style name. Yes, Indrid Cold. If you aren't sure of who Cold was (or, possibly, still is…), then just sit back and read. There's some amazing material coming. And it's coming quickly.

Sharing her time with me was a *very* cool thing Susan did. After that, I had to deliver my lecture at the local theater that was absolutely roasting hot inside. Me and Susan hugged, smiled and went our different ways. Matters weren't finished, though. About five days later, Susan sent me something amazing.

I don't know where else Susan went later that day. But I, know what I did: I gulped down a load of cold beer. I needed it by then. The sun was beating down on the city and the concrete was almost bleeding. And there was something else, too. Not long after, I got a thick document from Susan that – for me, at least – was akin to an Aladdin's Cave. The next night, I began to read. I have to say it was hard to stop. It was around 3:00 a.m. when I finally quit. I thought: tomorrow will be an exciting day. It was. This was important for all, not just for one. It was filled with incredible - and new - material on Mothman and more on Point Pleasant. Amazing secrets, too. So, with that said, let's see what Susan handed over to me...

CHAPTER 9:

IN A STATE OF COLD

The first piece of material that Susan gave me:

I may be one of the few people who remembers the West Virginia Mothman and related events before the "Mothman" even had a name. It was one chilly November day in 1966 that my sister came home from school to tell a peculiar story that happened the night before to Merle's Partridge's family. I was small at the time but I remember it this way: I sat at the kitchen table eating what remained of Halloween candy from the bottom of a grocery store bag. There was plastic over the kitchen windows to keep the cold out. The hill outside was covered with brown and yellow grass that seemed to ripple. It always seemed like there were presences in our woods. My sister burst through the front door-then told a story about Paula Partridge's Dad seeing red eyes in the barn the night before and that their German-Shepherd dog named Bandit was now missing.

Strange red eyes staring out of the doorway of an old barn wasn't something you heard about often in central West Virginia, so my childish mind was awakened and I held on to the story probably longer than anyone else in my family cared to. I can tell you that your ordinary West Virginia citizen didn't believe the tale at first. Until these strange manifestations that became Mothman, Indrid Cold and the Men in Black began to touch their lives in both big and small ways.

My family lived on Shannon's Knob in the small town of West Union, in Doddridge County, West Virginia while the Partridges lived about 8 miles away from us in a country community called Center Point, basically across a ridge or two. My grandmother had been the post mistress of Center Point where she grew up in a log cabin and there was even a Banshee story associated with the community. The dates that were given vary to some degree. It is usually accepted that the day of the Merle Partridge sighting - or the 'red eyes in the barn' - happened on November 15, 1966. It was the same night as the Scarberry encounter.

Shortly before 10 o'clock in the evening, Merle Partridge was watching late-night television with his son, Roger, who was about 11 years old at the time. They first noticed their German shepherd dog barking outside. It seemed to be at a distance from the house. They didn't really know, but they knew something was terribly wrong. And, at that very same time, the television set started 'screaming' as the picture blanked out and the TV made a loud grinding sound, which Mr. Partridge later told author John Keel, 'It sounded like a generator winding up.'

Partridge's account, which he told me in an interview in 2006, differed slightly than what John Keel eventually included in his *The Mothman Prophecies*. First, Keel must have misheard Merle Partridge's name and wrote it down as 'Newell Partridge.' Mr. Partridge was always open about the story and never asked to be given an alias. Merle Partridge told me, 'I don't know why John Keel wrote my name down as Newell.' It's possible the New York City author couldn't understand Partridge's West Virginia accent.

After listening to Bandit the dog bark for a little while longer, Merle Partridge decided it might be a good idea to investigate the noises. It could have been a prowler on his property or even a black bear; such a thing isn't impossible. Center Point was miles from any town. Mr. Partridge grabbed a flashlight, took Roger in tow and the two headed outdoors to find out what all of the ruckus was about. Partridge didn't see any red eyes from a distance, as some accounts claim. Instead, he saw Bandit standing at the entrance to the empty barn, which Partridge described as 'a football field away.' The dog barked frantically as he continued to stare into the barn.

As Merle Partridge and Roger got closer to the barn, Partridge said he felt the hair raise up on his arms. When he looked into the barn, he saw what he described as what looked to be, red, rotating electrical lights. Partridge explained to me, "Red lights, red eyes; whatever you want to call them."

On that chilly November night Partridge noticed what he thought was a dark shape lumbering up from the floor of the barn. The fur stood up on Bandit's back, the dog snarled angrily and he shot into the barn toward whatever the dark form was. Merle Partridge and Roger ran back to the house. As they sat down in front of the television set, Bandit stopped barking and the picture came back on the screen of the TV. Calm was restored. Still, Mr. Partridge later mentioned that he slept with his rifle beside of him that night. The next morning, Bandit did not come to the back door for his breakfast as he usually did. Merle Partridge remembered that the last time he'd seen Bandit, the dog was running into the barn seemingly in pursuit of the red eyes, or 'lights' and the dark form.

Merle and his children Mary, Roger and Gary headed for the barn and what they found inside was chilling and mysterious. They discovered Bandit's paw prints in the dirt floor of the barn, but the paw prints only went in a circle and didn't lead away. It was as if that dog had been picked up and carried away by something much stronger and larger. Mary Partridge also commented there were other tracks, but they didn't belong to the dog. She said they looked like giant turkey tracks, but ones like she'd never seen before.

At this point, Merle Partridge didn't realize that the night before - less than an hour after his encounter with the 'red eyes in the barn,' - Roger and Linda Scarberry, of Point Pleasant, along with Steve and Mary Mallette, would also meet up with these 'red eyes" at the TNT plant on the outskirts of town. They were able to see a figure attached to the red eyes or 'lights' in detail. It was a tall humanoid creature of over six feet tall, with crimson eyes that seemed to be set in its shoulders, and a wing span of almost 10 feet. (Later witnesses would describe the creature as varying shades of grey, brown or tan and sometimes flesh-toned.)

In later interviews, Linda Scarberry, like Merle Partridge, described the eyes of the creature as looking like 'red lights' and not really bicycle reflectors that Keel compares them to in his book. In fact, at one point when the Scarberry's thought they had outdistanced the Mothman after he had been flying over their car, Linda looked into a field and thought she saw red lights on a billboard. When the billboard was caught in the beams of the Scarberry's car, Linda claimed the Mothman was perched on the edge of the billboard. As they passed, the Mothman once again took flight and continued in pursuit of their car.

As they came upon the city limits of Point Pleasant, Linda Scarberry looked and saw the dead body of a large dog beside the road. As the young couple drove, the Mothman soared overhead but only a few feet above the car. The wings of the creature were so huge that as they flapped they hit the side doors of Roger's car. Once they arrived in town, they drove directly to the Point Pleasant Police Station and made their famous report. Sources say it was Roger Scarberry who made a sketch. When the police went out to check the car, they found large scratches on each side door.

When finally the frightened couple returned to their house, Linda Scarberry claimed the Mothman had followed them and peered into the windows the rest of the night. In one interview Linda remarked, 'Even to this day, I will not look out my windows after dark. Within a day or two, the Mothman story (the creature did not yet have a name and was referred to as a 'bird' or 'Birdman) made its way through news syndicates, appearing in newspapers but mostly in the mid-Atlantic region. These caught the eye of Merle Partridge in Doddridge County because the account seemed eerily similar to what he had experienced on the same night, but what he really noticed was the mention of the dead dog beside the city limits sign of Point Pleasant.

The Partridge's German shepherd dog, Bandit, did not return. Nor would he ever, sadly.

CHAPTER 10:

IT GETS EVEN COLDER

More words from Susan came tumbling out:

Strangeness that enveloped West Virginia and Ohio Valley did not begin with the Scarberry encounter along route 2 north of Point Pleasant. There had been another puzzling event that occurred in Parkersburg 12 days before. This happened on November 2, 1966 one mile south of the city limits of Parkersburg. It involved a sewing machine salesman whose life was about to be disrupted in such a way that he would never entirely recover.

His name was Woodrow Derenberger, but everyone called him "Woody." It was shortly after 6 p.m. in the evening, when Woody Derenberger was driving home from his job as a sewing machine salesman at J.C. Penny's in Marietta, Ohio to his farmhouse in Mineral Wells, West Virginia. The ride home was overcast and dreary. It was misting a light rain.

As Derenberger came up on the Intersection of I-77 and Route 47, he thought that a tractor trailer truck was tailgating him without its lights on, which was unnerving, so he swerved to the side of the road and much to his surprise, the truck appeared to take flight and seemed to roll across his panel truck. To his astonishment, what Derenberger thought was a truck was a charcoal colored UFO without any lights on. It touched down and then hovered about 10 inches above the berm of the road. Much to Derenberger's surprise a hatch opened and a man stepped out looking like any ordinary man you would see on the street - there was nothing unusual about his appearance.

Except the man was dressed in dark clothing and had a 'beaming smile.' As the man proceeded to walk toward Derenberger's panel truck the 'craft' jetted up to about 40 feet in the air where it floated above the highway. What happened next was unsettling, because as the darkly-dressed man came up toward the vehicle Woody Derenberger heard the words, "Do not be afraid, I mean you no harm, I only want to ask you a few questions." Derenberger did become afraid because as the man spoke to Woodrow his lips did not move. The man then moved to the opposite of the truck and told Derenberger to roll down his window so they could talk better, which he did. Next what formed in Derenberger's mind were the words, "Now you can speak, or you can think… it makes no difference, I can understand you either way,"

That was what the dark man said. Later, when Derenberger was questioned on local live television, he was scrutinized over what seemed a contradiction because if the dark man communicated through a type of mental telepathy, why would Derenberger need to roll down his window to talk? Wouldn't it be easier just to talk mentally?

Woodrow Derenberger explained it was because Indrid Cold wanted to look directly at him as they spoke and he felt that, really, Cold wasn't so interested in what was said but more interested in keeping up a communication with him. To Derenberger, that seemed the entire point of it all. Derenberger also noted that when Cold stared into his eyes, it was as if he knew everything about Woodrow Derenberger, and also, if he could only let go of his fear and do the same, he felt he would also know and understand all about Cold.

In any event, Cold spoke through the passenger side window the entire time. The physical description of Cold was commonplace. Derenberger described him as about 35 years of age, having a trim build, was about six feet tall, 185 pounds with dark eyes and dark hair slicked straight back. Cold wore a long dark coat and beneath the coat Woodrow Derenberger was able to glimpse the fabric of his "uniform" that glistened beneath the coat. He also described Cold as having a "tanned complexion." Throughout the conversation Cold kept a frozen smile and curiously hid his hands beneath his armpits most of the time.

At one point at the city lights above the distant hills of Parkersburg, Cold asked Mr. Derenberger, "What do you call that over there?" Derenberger said, "Why, that's Parkersburg and we call that a city." Cold responded, "Where I come from we call it a gathering." Cold later added the curious statement that "I come from a place less powerful than yours." As the men talked, cars passed under the craft which drifted above the road. The occupants

73

were seemingly unaware of the spaceship being there. After all, there were no lights that could be seen. Cold then asked about Parkersburg, "Do people live there or do they work there?"

Woody Derenberger answered, "Why, yes, people live and work there." Cold interjected: "Do you work, Mr. Derenberger?" (Woodrow told Cold his name as the conversation began) Derenberger answered, "I am a salesman. That's what I do. Do you have a job?" Cold answered, "Yes. I am a searcher." After that the conversation became mundane… Cold seemed to notice Woodrow Derenberger was scared and commented on it. Mr. Derenberger claimed Cold asked him, Why are you so frightened? Do not be afraid. We mean you no harm. You will see that we eat and bleed the same as you do," and then added an emotive note, "We only wish you happiness" which Cold said to the frightened man more than once.

While Mr. Derenberger was being interviewed on live television on WTAP-TV, he attributed this puzzling statement to Indrid Cold, 'At the proper time, the authorities will be notified about our meeting and this will be confirmed.' The entire conversation took between five and ten minutes and then Indrid Cold looked inside Woody's car with his ever-present smile, and said, 'Mr. Derenberger, I thank you for talking to me. We will see you again.'

He ended the conversation with 'We will see you again' and as soon as he did the spaceship immediately came back down, floated about 10 inches off the road. A hatch opened and a human arm extended pulling Cold up into the craft. The ship then jetted up into the air about seventy-five feet, made a fluttering noise and then shot away at a very high rate of speed. For a few moments, Woodrow Derenberger sat stunned. Finally, he started up his car and drove to his farmhouse in Mineral Wells where his wife met him at the door. By now it was shortly before 7:00 o'clock.

Mrs. Derenberger met her husband at the door. She later said that Woodrow "could not have been any whiter if he had been lying in a coffin.'" The stories vary but from Mr. Derenberger's account his wife is the one who called the West Virginia State police, or at least she dialed the phone. Woodrow Derenberger gave them a brief report of what he claimed to have happened. It is interesting to note that in the initial report, Derenberger called the alien "Cold," but did not mention "Indrid' until later."

The next day Derenberger attempted to go back to work but was sidetracked when he agreed to a live television interview about his experience on the previous night with a UFO with WTAP-TV the NBC affiliate in Parkersburg, housed in a small building not much bigger than a garage. The interview took place shortly before noon where Woodrow Derenberger was grilled by veteran reporter Glenn Wilson and city Police Chief Ed Plum as well as other local law enforcement including the head of the Wood County Airport. Representatives from Wright Patterson were in route to interview Derenberger but whether that came about is not known.

The interview went on for about two and a half hours. The live part of the broadcast was under an hour long and then the television cameras were turned off, and the interview continued off the air for another hours or so. During that time, Derenberger drew a picture of the spacecraft which he described in his thick West Virginia accent as a charcoal grey, with no lights and looking like an 'old-fashioned chimney lamp.' (You may want to google this because I am not clear what he intended. I found some interesting images when I did…Parts of the lamps may look like UFOs.)

Probably one of the most curious statements Woodrow Derenberger made about his meeting with Cold was, "And then Cold said to me, we will see you again…" then his voice trails off. Police Chief Ed Plum asked, "Do you really believe you will see him again?" Derenberger then answered, 'I think so… I believe I will… I don't know… because that's what I am afraid of.

After that interview, Derenberger's life transformed drastically and not for the better. He changed jobs, developed marital problems, clung to his church for a while, and then came the strange visits from men dressed in black clothing whom Derenberger suspected to be some kind of hidden government group of spies or maybe even the Mafia. He wasn't sure, they just spooked him. They would arrive his house, ask Derenberger simple questions, (some had to do with his UFO experience) and then the Men in Black acted in a threatening manner.

But nothing was as incredible as the return of Indrid Cold. At least, this is what Woodrow Derenberger claimed. He said that Cold visited him many times at his farmhouse in Mineral Wells. At one point, Derenberger came up missing for almost six months and said he was "with the aliens." The local population finally became skeptical. The sewing machine salesman's tale grew more and more far-fetched. Derenberger even claimed to have been impregnated by the aliens. In 1967, Woodrow Derenberger stated to have visited Indrid Cold's home planet of Lanulos where its residents walked around wearing no clothing. He said the aliens lived in a galaxy called Ganymede where everything was peaceful and there was no war. People began to snicker.

Still, there were odd flashing lights in the sky almost nightly and the curiosity seekers stalked not only Derenberger's modest farmhouse, but an area called Bogle Ridge, not far from Mineral Wells where the aliens were claimed to land. The ridicule became too much. Derenberger, with his family, moved from the area and stayed away for decades. He returned to Wood County in the 1980s and died in 1990. Woodrow Derenberger was finally laid to rest at Mount Zion Cemetery in Mineral Wells, West Virginia.

John Keel was not a believer in Woodrow Derenberger's UFO story so it's mysterious why he would make it such a big part of *The Mothman Prophecies* book. In *The Mothman Prophecies* movie the character Gordon Smallwood is based upon Woodrow Derenberger but the Wood County man most often appeared in a suit and not overalls. A few elements to his story make it believable that, initially, something of an extraordinary nature, happened to him. First of all, his account predates the Mothman sightings by 12 days. Derenberger would have had to have been a prophet to know what was about to happen next, making his story even more extraordinary. His family explains that they believe something of an otherworldly nature initially happened but he added to the tale to sell books when he self-published a book called *Visitors from Lanulos* in 1971.

There are a few other accounts that add some believability to key aspects of Woodrow Derenberger's fantastic story. An elderly man driving south of Parkersburg on I-77 reported seeing a man by the side of the road (one that meet Indrid Cold's description) who tried to flag him down. The gentleman slowed down but when the darkly-clad man headed for the passenger door of his car, the senior citizen became frightened and drove away. 'There was something off about that character,' the old man later told Glenn Wilson of WTAP-TV.

I also ran into something curious when I was researching stories for my ghost tour back in 1996. I found the news article about Woodrow Derenberger's UFO tale in the Parkersburg *News & Sentinel* dated November 4th, 1966 where the story was on a front section of the newspaper. The account read '"Local Man Stopped by UFO." In the same section of the newspaper, right beside of it, was another smaller article about a complete power outage that happened in South Parkersburg at precisely the same time Derenberger claimed he was interrupted by Indrid Cold's spaceship. South Parkersburg borders the community of Mineral Wells. An energy disturbance in Mineral Wells would likely also affect South Parkersburg.

CHAPTER 11:

"MY GRANDFATHER AND HIS HUGE BALL OF LIGHT"

We had hardly begun when Susan was
giving me mountains of material

My grandfather, W. P. Chapman of Cairo, West Virginia in Ritchie County, worked as a signal man for the B & O Railroad. In the fall of 1966, he was checking signal lights late one night outside of Cairo that weren't working properly. He was driving on Park Road near Cairo when suddenly what looked to be a fiery ball of light came up behind his truck rapidly. As the ball of light rolled across top of his truck, the power went out and the truck rolled down into a dark field. My grandfather's vehicle was completely drained of its power. The ball of light flew forward then disappeared into the blackness of the night sky. As the ball was out of sight, the power in his truck came back on. Unnerved, my grandfather drove on to check the signal lights which now appeared to work even though before the lights had been reported broken.

In late February of 1967, my grandfather was sitting at his desk in Cairo in front of a large window. As my grandmother passed behind his chair, she noticed three bright lights in the evening sky, red, white and green. They blinked on and off at different times, then disappeared.

A few weeks later, my grandfather was again checking faulty signal lights. Unfortunately, he suffered a heart attack on the train tracks and was unable to get out of the path of an oncoming train. My grandfather was killed. My West Virginia grandmother later described the lights in the sky as 'tokens' or warnings of his death, but UFOs that were proliferating in the nighttime skies were much more likely.

In late winter of 1967 a church bus was driving over Route 50 that then went directly through the small town of West Union, where I was raised. The occupants of the bus noticed on nearby Shannon's Knob that a UFO was hovering over my family's home. Shannon's Knob was the hillside I grew up on and the highest point in the town. A woman who was a passenger on the bus called my parents to tell them about the spacecraft suspended over our home but my parents were disbelieving.

The following spring my friend Regina Ball and I were playing on the hillside above my family's house. At the peak of Shannon's Knob was the entire power source for the town of West Union. We walked up a hill near a clearing to play "Indians" like we always did. As Jeanie and I played, we suddenly heard men's voices. Turning, we saw two men dressed in black near the rise above us. We were frolicking near the bushes but when we noticed the Men in Black we became scared and hid. We watched silently as the two men measured a spot on the hillside.

The men exuded an uncanny energy which I immediately sensed. They also looked differently from each other. One man appeared to be of European descent while the other one had an East Asian appearance. The one with the Asian appearance had what looked to be dyed blond hair that was cut very short. Neither was wearing a hat, nor did they wear a suit and tie. They simply had on a black shirt and black pants. The men seem interested only in the landscape and spoke to each other in low voices. Jeanie and I spied on the two men until they left. There was no vehicle anywhere close.

Where they came from, we did not know. Jeanie and I went home and forgot all about them. In years to come, we would both suffer from migraine headaches and just overall poor health. We never linked the Men in Black up on the hill with our headaches. I later learned Derenberger suffered from severe headaches as did his daughter.

A few days after some boys were playing on the same hillside. The boys noticed a circular impression in the grass that was about 15-20 feet wide in a treeless area on Shannon's Knob. They went home and reported it to their parents. My brother came home from school relaying the story from his friends. In my child's mind, I made the connection. It was almost like a secret that only I was privy to. To my knowledge, no one ever followed up on the circular impression on Shannon's Knob nor the UFO sighting over our house.

In the winter and spring of 1967, when my grandfather

was hit and killed by a train and we witnessed the Men in Black up on Shannon's Knob, we had other bizarre happenings. Our home became an epicenter for poltergeist activity. Ceramic birds flew off our living room mantle. Pictures fell off the walls. A heavy iron was tossed from my bedroom into the bedroom of my parents and slid under the bed where my Dad was sleeping.

But nothing was quite as strange as the footsteps I heard walking on the roof at night. This was the winter of 1967 and for the most part, appearances of these footsteps went on for as long as up until 1970. On certain nights, around 2:00 a.m. a loud bang would punctuate the stillness of my bedroom. It originated from the roof above me. It sounded like someone had jumped out of a helicopter onto our roof with a boom. There would be a pause of a few moments, and then, whoever it was, began to walk on the roof. The roof would creak under the weight. If I would scream for my parents, which I did often, the footsteps would pause until it grew quiet again and they would start right back up.

At first my parents did not believe me. However, one morning I heard them talking amongst themselves. My parents had heard the footsteps on the roof as well. I began to sleep walk. Sometimes I would wake up to hear the radio playing what sounded like a Catholic Mass but there were no active Catholic churches in my town. I reached over to turn off the radio and found that the radio wasn't on. Then I would lie there and listen to a "broadcast" of an "angel choir" with no source for the music until the cords faded as the sun finally came up.

One morning I woke up in a different bedroom that my family never used with a sheet pulled over my head like I was a dead person on a gurney ready to be taken to the morgue. As I stirred from sleep, I felt my skin had grown cold against the clammy air and realized every stitch of my clothing had been removed. I had no idea how I got there nor why my clothes had been taken off me. Embarrassed, I jumped from the bare bed, put my clothes on and never told a soul. My parents were sleeping normally in theirs. I was seven years old. Perhaps the strangest tale of all was one about our house more than a decade before we moved in. A young woman was babysitting at what would later be our home.

She thought she heard something attempting to climb up the side wall of the house. Too frightened to go check for herself, the girl called the West Union city police. When cops came to check the house, they were shocked when their flashlights shone up the side of the wall. There were muddy footprints traveling up the side of the house. Whether they were human or something else, that part I don't know. From then on our house became known as one that was haunted in town. But by what?

CHAPTER 12:

IT DIDN'T END THERE FOR MERLE PARTRIDGE

*More papers and documents on Mothman
and Cold surfaced from Susan*

Merle Partridge and Woodrow Derenberger had a number of things in common. Both were every day working family men with unexceptional lives until the month of November 1966. Derenberger was a sewing machine salesman and Merle Partridge worked as a truck driver. After going through such mysterious occurrences, each man's life turned the page to a new chapter of high strangeness.

Merle Partridge never sought the limelight in the same way Woody Derenberger did. He made his report to the news syndicate and was later interviewed by *Mothman Prophecies'* author John Keel and that was it. Partridge was done with the story. Keel took some liberties with Partridge's account. First, he wrote "Merle" as "Newell: in the book, which Partridge never fully understood. Partridge also thought the 'red eyes' actually looked more like red lights that rotated and circled not like bicycle reflectors that Keel put in the book. Lastly, Partridge lived at Center Point and not nearby Salem, although Salem may have been Partridge's mailing address.

In 2006 I interviewed Merle Partridge. He didn't have much to add to the initial story of Bandit and the red orbs in the barn other than what had been published, and as it was with most Mothman accounts, what happened to Partridge was memorable but very brief. Except for the stories that came later. Merle claimed that in the spring following his experience in November he was lying out on the deck of his house relaxing when suddenly the sky darkened. He looked up to see a dark grey spacecraft moving soundlessly above him. He saw no flashing lights but said the craft was so enormous that it cast a shadow over him and the house. Partridge also claimed the UFO made no noise whatsoever and that it was gone within minutes.

It wasn't but a few weeks later that Partridge had a knock on his door around 9:00 p.m. He opened the door to find a middle-aged man who was clearly upset. The man explained he had run his jeep into a ditch a few minutes before but that wasn't what he was worried about. He said he could not find his six year old son who had been sitting in the car seat beside of him. The man said as the two drove down the dark country road, something dark flew over and blocked out the view through his windshield. The next thing the man knew his Jeep was sitting in a ditch and his son was missing from the passenger seat.

First thing Merle Partridge and the man did was go out searching for the six-year old with flashlights but the boy was nowhere to be found. Partridge then dialed the

Salem police department and they made it to the farmhouse within a half hour. With two policemen they once
again embarked to search the country road and grounds
where the boy came up missing. Much to their surprise, the
young lad came down the road in the opposite direction
of where he and his father were traveling. It was if the boy
was sleep-walking. When the father shook him and asked
him where he had gone? The boy had no recollection of
where he had been for the almost hour and a half. The
night ended in both a relief and a mystery.

About thirty-five years later a man who looked to be
about forty years old knocked on the door. By this time,
Mr. Partridge and his wife were living in New Martinsville,
which is 100 miles upriver from Point Pleasant. The man
introduced himself by a name that was not familiar and
then said to Merle Partridge, "I know you don't recognize
me but I was the boy that got lost after our Jeep went off
the road that night thirty-five years ago and you helped
find me. To this day I have no memory whatsoever of
that hour I was lost."

The last story Merle Partridge told me did not disap-
point in its peculiarity. Most of his life was spent as a truck
driver. Mr. Partridge was on a particularly long drive, it
was a foggy morning and he made it almost home when
he was overcome by a terrible fatigue. He decided to pull
over and get a few winks in the cab of his truck. After
sleeping for a few hours, Mr. Partridge finally awoke to
a sticky feeling on his hands and face. As he opened his
eyes, he was shocked to find that his body was covered
in cobwebs.

That ended the stories Merle Partridge told me in 2006. He was featured in the movie *Eyes of the Mothman* along with other Mothman witnesses but passed away before ever seeing himself on the silver screen. Merle Partridge was a kind and intelligent man who never sought out attention or special treatment. I believed all that he said.

CHAPTER 13:

THE DERENBERGER TAPES - AND ENTER BILLI

Susan reeled out the tapes for me. I listened carefully.

I gave monthly live horoscopes and astrology segments on WTAP-TV in Parkersburg for a number of years, and knew Glenn Wilson, the man who had interviewed Woodrow Derenberger in November of 1966. When Glenn retired around 2001 he had something he thought I might like to have – they were the original reel-to-reel tapes of his live interview with Derenberger on November 3rd, 1966. These were audio tapes of more than two hours long and on them was written 'UFO TAPES November 1966.

Wilson almost threw them away, he told me, because he felt Derenberger had given Parkersburg a "black-eye," having made the city a laughing stock over his alien visits and extraterrestrial pregnancy claims. Wilson said there was also video of the live interview and a drawing Derenberger had produced of Indrid Cold's spaceship but both came up missing. Wilson assumed the cleaning lady had threw them out with the garbage.

The infamous UFO interview had not been listened to for about thirty-five years and hearing them for the first time was quite remarkable. Musician and Emmy winner David Traugh, who owned a recording studio in Parkersburg, transferred the rare interview to a cassette tape in summer of 2001. Woodrow Derenberger had come back to life to tell his story all over again. One could hear him rap his knuckles on the table during the interview for emphasis and listen as he faltered a bit. Yet Mr. Derenberger was consistent in everything he said.

Later, I burned the interviews on to a CD and presented them to author John Keel in 2003 at the only Mothman Festival (held each year in Point Pleasant) he attended. He commented that he didn't even know the interviews existed and seemed skeptical that they were real. I assured him they were genuine and I hoped he would enjoy them. The last thing John Keel said to me was, 'I hope you make some money off of these.'

However, before all of this, in 2001, I was doing book-signing for my own astrology book. Then, a young man in a long dark coat appeared at the bookstore. He was dressed in dark clothing and was about six feet tall with dark hair combed straight back. He had a medium build and dark eyes. The man appeared to be in his mid-thirties and he introduced himself as Billi.

Billi was very good-looking. In fact, he resembled the actor Richard Gere – who was the star of the movie version of *The Mothman Prophecies* - and I thought he had a Slavic or part-Native American appearance. It was now August of 2001, so it was time to begin preparation for my seasonal ghost tour. And that meant putting a new message on my answering machine. One night I walked in to find my answering machine's red light blinking, and played back the message which turned out to be a hissing voice saying the word 'Hi!' But the word was drawn out and the raspy greeting sounded more along the lines of: "Hiiiiiiiiiii-eeeeeeeee-yaaaaaaaah!" It was really a long hiss. I'm used to prank calls, so I deleted the recorded message and carried on. But there was something about this voice that didn't seem exactly human."

CHAPTER 14:

SUSAN AND BILLI

An inhuman voice and Susan tells all

In the following weeks a catastrophe would hit the United States. On September 11, 2001 the World Trade Center in NYC, Shanksville, PA and the Pentagon were attacked and 2,996 innocent individuals lost their lives. Like most Americans, I tried to move past my own shock and fulfill my obligations, and that would be preparing for another ghost tour coming up in little over a month. I thought, maybe, one new twist on the ghost tour might help. It would not only be an escape for everyone, but also entertaining. In late 2001, aliens, as well as ghosts, were now pretty low on the list of scares.

The 2001 fall season grew cold rather quickly and tour-goers were soon wearing winter coats in October. One night, I looked over as I told the Indrid Cold story. And, I was about to play the Derenberger tapes to the crowd when I glimpsed a man dressed in a long and dark coat who stood apart from the rest of the crowd. It was Billi. Not only that, I had a feeling that Billi was also someone else – Indrid Cold.

Absorbed in my stories, Billi remained polite through-out the evening and trailed behind at the end of the crowd. Back at the hotel as the tour ended, Billi said, "I like the way you tell stories." Then he disappeared through the hotel's front doors. I watched through the window as Billi paused at the wait-and-walk sign outside and then crossed the street in the chilled, fall air. Billi attended the ghost tour about two or three times that season. He was always quiet and he was always alone. I had a feeling that I should share: Billi was from Cold's planet.

In November of 2001, a phone call woke me up about 2 a.m. I recognized the voice. It was the same raspy voice that left a message on my answering machine earlier, with the exact same message: "Hiiiiiiiiiii-eeeeeeeee-yaaaaaaaah!" (As in Hi!) The inhuman voice unnerved me so I slammed the receiver down, but instantly regretted it. Perhaps, I could find out who was pranking me.

"Curiosity got the best of me, so I did a *69, which, in this area of the country, means this will give you the num-ber that last called. I don't remember the exact number, but I immediately found out the number was from a Point Pleasant, West Virginia line. I only know two residents of Point Pleasant well enough to call me on the telephone: Jeff Wamsley of the Mothman Museum (and festival) and my brother-in-law's sister. The number belonged to neither of them. I decided I would risk being rude. So, I dialed the number even though it was past 2 a.m. All I had to do was punch the #1 on my phone as a call back and the phone would ring. I must admit, I was not surprised when an electronic voice clicked on and said,

"The number you have called has been disconnected and is no longer in service." Yet, the number had called me just five minutes earlier.

I sat down in my chair, shaken. There were perceptions in the back of my mind I knew I had been repressing. Because I considered them impossible. I thought of the appearances of Billi and how he said he had been born in November of 1966. That Mothman surfaced in 1966. And how Billi fit perfectly the description of Indrid Cold, with his long dark coat, his tanned complexion and his hair combed straight back. And if Billie really was Cold, he had not aged and still remained at 35 years old. There was not a wrinkle on his face. I also remember how diligently Billi had listened to the Woodrow- Derenberger tapes as if he had a secret, but never commented on it. However, this might all be just an overwhelming coincidence. I didn't think so, though.

On Thanksgiving weekend of each year, the local Smoot Theater features a production of *A Christmas Carol* that is put on by the Missoula Theater of Nebraska. It's a grand show which local people look forward to attending year after year. My family, at the time, was no exception. We looked forward to attending on the Friday night presentation in 2001. Thanksgiving was, as always, a Thursday. My family had good seats, and we waited as other members of the audience filled the theater. To my right, was my then-husband and to my left was an empty chair that was an aisle seat. While my eyes scanned the darkened theater, I then heard a slick rustling and noticed someone sat down beside of me. I turned. It was Billi.

The dark-dressed man, who now seemed almost a friend, squirmed in his seat and before the play was over, Billi left. After the play had concluded, my ten-year-old daughter commented that she noticed Billi's long, black coat was made out of an unusual material like the water-proof fabric on a tent. This was no normal man.

Nick Redfern at the Mothman Festival

*Point Pleasant's
incredible stainless steel
creation of Mothman*

One of today's huge bridges at Point Pleasant

Nick hanging out with the late Susan Sheppard

The banner that stands over the city every year

Jon Downes: Owl-Man expert

*Norka's painting
of the red-eyed
creature she saw
in Puerto Rico's El
Yunque forest*

*Mothman
at night*

*Rosemary
Ellen Guiley:
Djinn expert*

*Susan Sheppard
chatting with me
about Mothman
and Indrid Cold*

The Mothman Museum: not to be missed

CHAPTER 15:

"MY FRIEND'S EYES DARTED BACK AND FORTH"

Susan has more to say – and even more

Local art association, *Artsbridge*, used to put on what was called their 'Chair Auction' where area artists painted used furniture that was auctioned off to help their organization with funding in art education. Not a bad idea. I was one of the local artists invited to paint a piece of furniture, which I did. I painted an old telephone stand with a Halloween theme and even added a ceramic vintage pumpkin; it looked like a dreaming, sleeping child. This would have been late summer of 2002. On the night of the auction, we assembled at the local Art Center to enjoy the refreshments and watch our art pieces being auctioned off. I was sitting with my friend, whose grandson had just had brain surgery for their Chiari Syndrome. It was not long after 9/11 and everyone needed a lift.

As the second floor banquet room of the Art Center began to fill with people, I noticed Billi, in his dark coat, enter the room. But he wasn't alone. Billi arrived with a surreal-looking blond companion over six-feet- tall with pointy, cone-like breasts. Wearing a shade of bright coral lipstick, the woman resembled a late 1950s to early 1960s pin-up model. She was dressed mostly in black. I also felt this girl could be from Indrid Cold's world.

I poked my friend and commented, 'That's Billi!' I pointed in their direction. My friend's eyes widened and you would have thought she was looking at the chain-rattling ghost of Ebenezer Scrooge. But, it was Billi, all right, and he wasn't a ghost. The auction began. Soon, my art piece came up for bids. The bidding grew fast and heated. My friend's eyes darted back and forth. And then her gaze fixed on me.

"He's bidding on you," she whispered. "I dared not look."

Not surprising, Billi was the highest bidder and bought my Halloween-themed, vintage telephone stand. I was stunned for the third or fourth time. When was this going to end? My friend had the composure to go downstairs where items were being paid for. So, she followed Billi and his blond bombshell to the check-out area. My friend came back upstairs and said to me, "Susan, Billi paid for your art in cash. He then clasped the stand to his chest and ran out of the Art Center as if he scored some great prize."

"After this, I never saw Billi again. It makes me wonder if my art is now being looked upon with quizzical stares by humanoids dressed in black, far, far away in a galaxy called Ganymede, on a planet named Lanulos. Perhaps, a place that is 'less powerful that yours' … one inhabited by a guy called 'Billi' or maybe even 'Indrid Cold.' I don't know…However, the strangeness that visited my life wasn't over quite yet."

CHAPTER 16:

WEIRD PHONE CALLS AND MEN IN BLACK APPEARANCES

Susan gets mysterious callers and tells
me of the M.I.B. and more

If you have read John Keel's *The Mothman Prophecies* book, or watched the movie starring Richard Gere, you already know that both Indrid Cold and the Men in Black have a fascination with phones. Their calls are usually creepy. Or, they seem to have a way of letting us know they are watching us. And are aware of what we are saying or doing. Maybe both. There is a lot of paranoia with those phones and the voices at the other end. It doesn't frighten me anymore. But, it does fascinate me.

Haunted Parkersburg tour guide, Virginia Lyons, attended a Mothman festival with me a year or two after the Billi appearances. Virginia, at the time, was a dedicated home health aide. She had never had any Men in Black experiences. But, she *was* a small child when the Mothman appearances happened: the Woodrow Derenberger UFO encounter. Remembering and watching his live television

MOTHMAN & OTHER FLYING MONSTERS

interview. Virginia was also the neighbor of Woodrow
Derenberger's niece, who lived across the street from
her and her husband Steve. Held in mid-September the
annual Mothman festival occurs in what is usually the last
hot weekend of the year. West Virginia's seasons change
quickly, but the Mothman festival is typically sweltering,
making it hard on the actors portraying MIBs, who walk
around in black suits that are much too hot for the season.

We were having a late Saturday dinner at a restaurant
when we were interrupted by phone calls. Virginia had just
purchased a new cell phone, which she used to keep tabs
on any of her patients. One was having some problems
at the time, and even though Virginia had not yet figured
out all of the bells and whistles on her new phone, she
kept it close by for emergencies.

After we ordered our dinner, Virginia's phone rang.
She picked it up. No one spoke, but the phone gave off
a muffled, underwater sound. She put the phone down
and within minutes it rang again. The call back number
was 111-111-1111. She had never heard of the number
before. Nor did it exist; except in some weird hoaxes
involving a certain newspaper. But, this was well before
2011. Because I'd just given a talk on Indrid Cold and the
Men in Black, we guffawed and joked. I commented, "It
must be Indrid Cold. He knows we're here." The phone
rang a few more times and Virginia tried to check her
voice-mail, but she hadn't figured it out yet. The evening
was otherwise uneventful. And on Sunday, Virginia
and I returned to Parkersburg after another fun-filled
Mothman festival.

"The next day Virginia called me. She had figured out her new phone. Someone had left a voice mail for her and she warned me, "Sit down. You are not going to believe this. Let me play it for you." She then played her message and once again there was the strange, rasping voice I recognized saying 'Hiiiiiiiiiii-eeeeeeeee-yaaaaaaaah' on Virginia's voice mail. It was the same inhuman voice. Which again, we took to mean "Hi." But, behind that "Hi" there seemed to be a message that was meant to unnerve and possibly threaten us, the listeners.

After that, I stopped speaking about Indrid Cold and the Men in Black on the *Haunted Parkersburg Ghost Tours*. Not because I was scared. But, because it seemed people would rather listen to ghost stories. Even though the Indrid Cold story happened mostly in the Parkersburg area, the interest did not seem to be there for the strange UFO tale any longer. I also think a part of me didn't want to see Billi again. And I feared he might come back to me. And on top, the Men in Black weren't done with me yet. I just knew it. I was in a world of M.I.B., Mothman, Indrid Cold and more. It was all melting together.

CHAPTER 17:

THE M.I.B. JUST WON'T GO AWAY

Now, we're getting to the end of
Susan's epic adventures:

In 2006 my mother had an operation on her esophagus that went terribly wrong. She lingered in the hospital and nursing homes until 2009. That was when she finally died. During her time in the hospital, my sister often stayed with her. One afternoon, while I was napping, my sister heard a rap on the front-door. She opened it to see two men dressed in black, who seemed eager to talk for some reason. Thinking they were fundamentalist Christians, or holy rollers, from a local church, my sister asked them what they wanted. The men asked, "Is Susan at home?"

My sister answered, "Yes, but she is upstairs, sleeping." The two men dressed in black didn't seem satisfied with the answer and appeared to crane their necks to look inside the house as if they were searching for some glimpse of me. They stood for a few moments in awkward silence. One looked at the other and then back at my sister. "Susan is sleeping?" he asked.

My sister said, "Yes, our mother is sick and Susan is very tired."

The men, again, seemed to grasp for words. As my sister looked behind them, she saw two *other* men dressed in black across the street, standing as if they were waiting on the two men staring in the house.   Finally, the one man at the door said, "Please tell Susan we were here. We hope she feels better. We will see her again."

The two men dressed in black walked down from the cement steps to my house. They joined the remaining two men. It was a non-descript black car, and all four men were dressed in black. They drove away without any kind of fanfare in sight. They did not seem to be interested in visiting any other home. That was ten years ago and it was my last encounter with any Men in Black. To my relief, Billi has never reappeared. I would think if he had been just a local resident, I would have seen him again, over and over. But, such a thing never has happened. Billi completely vanished from my life, and as mysteriously as he arrived. However, I plan to add the Men in Black and Indrid Cold in the Haunted Parkersburg tours in 2017. And by playing those old UFO tapes. It's very likely Billie and the Men in Black will return. Frankly, I'd be surprised if they didn't.

My last thought about all of this is that Billie and Indrid Cold were the very same entities. Does this mean Billie/Indrid Cold was an immortal? After all, he was around from the 1960s and never aged.

Susan finished her massive story on August 28, 2017. That's when she handed over her document to me.

Susan died on April 19, 2021. What an incredible body of work she left behind her. It will never be forgotten. Something else: there was much more about 2017; *much more*. Something that was both incredible and terrifying. I mean about nightmares, prophecies, Mothman and a nuclear war – and not just around the Point Pleasant area. Rather, all over the place: *the planet, even.*

CHAPTER 18:

FLYING HUMANS OR GIANT BIRDS?

EITHER WAY IT'S INCREDIBLE!

It wasn't long before I was looking into yet another winged humanoid – and all thanks to Susan, who had a growing interest in the similarities between Mothman and what are known as the Bird People of Brazil. Again, I placed all the material into my various archives:

> San Antonio, Texas-based cryptozoologist, Ken Gerhard, is one of the world's leading seekers of strange creatures. His investigations have taken him, quite literally, across the globe, as he has pursued the likes of the Chupacabra, werewolves, Bigfoot, and lake monsters. Ken notes:
>
> One of the greatest experiences of my life was traveling throughout the continent of South America when I was but a lad. My mother, who had been in remission from cancer at the time, had a newfound zeal for life and wanted to expose me and my sister to faraway lands and new experiences. Among the wonders that we were fortunate enough to see were the lofty and mysterious Inca

ruins of Machu Picchu in the Andes Mountains, as well as the diverse natural wonders of the Galapagos Islands.

One of Ken's favorite memories from that time is of an adventure along the Amazon River, deep within the dense and mysterious jungle environment. It was while there that Gerhard, his mother, and sister were introduced to the people of the Javaro and Yagua tribes, who remained blissfully unchanged by the technological and high-stress-based world of the final years of the 20ᵗʰ century.

Ken noted: "Surely, if there is anywhere on the planet where strange, new creatures lurk, the Green Continent just might be the place." He was not wrong.

Ken has investigated a curious story that occurred back in the 1950s; the location being southern Brazil, specifically close to Pelotas, a coastal city. It involved two witnesses, Luiz de Rosario Real and his wife, Lucy Gerlach Real. As they casually walked along an enchanting forested path, they saw what appeared to be two large birds, silhouetted in the Moon-dominated sky. As the "birds" got closer, however, the dumbstruck pair could see that the creatures were not birds, after all, but winged humanoids. When the beasts realized they had been seen they retreated into the dense, surrounding trees. That was scarcely the end of things, however: both husband and wife, as they exited the area with speed, developed a strong and disturbing feeling that the winged monsters were stalking them. Whether to make a meal of them or not, we will never know. They suddenly soared into the skies above, never to be seen again. It was, perhaps, a lucky escape for Luiz and Lucy.

CHAPTER 19:

KONGAMATO!

"SWOOPING DOWN!"

I should note that while I was still digging into my research into the matter of Mothman, I was also delving into the history of the African version of the creature; something that's not too different from the Mothman. "Fuck, I thought! These creatures are all over the place!" Yep, they're here, there and everywhere. As I note below:

> The continent of Africa is the reported home of numerous unknown creatures and wild monsters. They range from goliath-sized ape-men to lake-monsters and from dinosaur-like lizards to massive spiders, as we shall see later. Africa is also the domain of more than a few large, winged, flying monsters. A wealth of such stories comes from the Bokaonde and Kaonde tribes of Zambia. It's largely thanks to an early 20th century explorer, Frank H. Melland, that we know of the accounts of these immense and fearsome fliers. Melland's sources in the tribes told him that the most feared of all the monsters of the skies was the Kongamato. Its name means 'over-whelmer [sic]

of boats.' The name is a very apt one, since it had the habit of swooping down on canoes and savagely attacking and killing those within. It was a huge beast that lived in, and hunted in, the Jiundu swamps, and which deeply terrified the people of the area.

As for the appearance of the Kongamato, it looked somewhat like a bird – at first glance. That it utterly lacked feathers, however, and the fact that its red body was leathery-looking, was membranous, and had wings far more befitting those of a bat, suggests it was something else entirely. Moreover, its immense mouth was filled with sharp teeth that could slice a man in two in an instant, which is not something typical of the average bird.

Acting purely on instinct, when Melland explored the area in 1924 – a trip which he chronicled in his 1923 book, *In Witchbound Africa* – he showed the local tribes-people artistic renditions of various presumed extinct pterosaurs, including one of a pterodactyl. On seeing the pictures, the tribespeople cried one word, and one word only: 'Kongamato!

Very likely connected to the tales told by the Bokaonde and Kaonde tribes are similar accounts coming out of the Kitui Wakamaba people, also of Zambia. They told their stories to a man named A. Blayney Percival who, in 1928, penned *A Game Ranger on Safari*. So the Kitui Wakamaba said, they could always tell when one of the chiefly nocturnal creatures had landed near their villages, as they always left behind them, large, telltale tracks on the ground. As with the data shared with Frank H. Melland a few years earlier, the Kitui Wakamba described their resident monster as large, leathery and possessed of huge, membranous wings. Such stories were also handed to, and faithfully recorded by, Colonel Charles R.S Pitman, the author of *A Game Warden Takes Stock*. On top of that, a well-respected ichthyologist, Dr. J.L.B. Smith, investigated a number of almost identical cases from Tanzania's Mount Kilimanjaro.

If one takes a trip along Africa's Gold Coast, one is likely to eventually come across stories of the Susabonsam. To the locals, it very much resembles something that is half-man and half-bat. It's notable that a revered crypto-zoologist, Ivan Sanderson, wrote in his book, *Investigating the Unexplained*, that while wading in an African creek at some point in 1932, he was suddenly, and out of the blue, dive-bombed by an immense creature with a wingspan of around twelve feet. As someone well acquainted with just about every animal under the sun, Sanderson knew exactly what the beast was. It was a bat, although one of previously unheard of, massive proportions. The precise location was Cameroon's Assumbo Mountains. And Sanderson was not alone; also witness to the obscenely huge bat was a biologist named Gerald Russell, who shot at the animal but failed to kill it.

It was this close call with death that led Sanderson to ponder on an intriguing possibility. He began to wonder if the Kongamato, the Susabonsam, and a variety of other flying monsters reported in Africa were not surviving pterosaurs, after all. He came to believe that each and every one of them may have been examples of giant, ferocious bats. In many respects, this makes a great deal of sense.

After all, the idea of giant bats is far more plausible than surviving pockets of animals believed to have become extinct tens of millions of years ago.

CHAPTER 20:

2017: MOTHMAN AND AN APOCALYPTIC SITUATION

The year 2017 was an important one. A *very* important one. A disturbing one, too. Check out the date: a 50th anniversary for the Mothman phenomenon. There were deep worries about nuclear war – and on a global level, no less. North Korea was shouting and threatening to launch nukes into the skies. "Little Kim" was bragging and ranting he could launch nuclear missiles into the United States' airspace. As just about all the media noted, Chicago, Illinois was a prime key target for America. People were saying this really *was* the end. For a while, *I* thought there was going to be – at the *very* least – localized nuclear attacks on the U.S. And, of course, that really would have been the end of it all, as a war like that would grow and grow. Thankfully, it didn't happen.

There was, however, *something else*, too; it was something that was both terrifying and paranormal: as the threats of nuclear war grew and grew, more and more people were having nightmares and prophecies in the dead of the night. Most of those dreams revolved around Mothman and gigantic, radioactive mushroom clouds. Many people generously shared their dreams with me. The anniversary prompted something else, too: a pair of new

115

books about the subject of Mothman. One of the books was Lon Strickler's *Mothman Dynasty: Chicago's Winged Humanoids*. Lon said of his book:

IT SEEMED LIKE THE NUKES WERE READY TO HIT THE RED BUTTON AND LAUNCH

"In the late summer of 2011, three reports of Mothman-like flying humanoids surfaced in the city of Chicago, then nothing. Whatever it was disappeared. Then unexpectedly in early 2017, a smattering of encounters emerged from different locations throughout the Chicago metro area. These reports quickly grew to nearly fifty before stopping suddenly at the end of the summer. Why Chicago? Why now? This book will examine the witness accounts as well as the investigators thought processes in real time as these incidents were brought to our attention.

The sightings continue... but we are determined to find the truth."

The other book was *The Lake Michigan Mothman: High Strangeness in the Midwest*. The author was Tobias Wayland, who said of his book: "This book represents over two years of research by a dedicated team of investigators who have taken dozens of reports of a weird, winged humanoid seen around Lake Michigan. Author and investigator Tobias Wayland has collected these reports for the first time in one volume, along with his analysis and insider perspective as a member of the investigative team. The phenomena described the continuation of a decades-long series of events first recorded in Point Pleasant, West Virginia, in the late '60s, but that has likely been with humanity since our advent, and seems just as likely to be with us until our end."

Things were, indeed, expanding – and most definitely not in a good way. That red-eyed thing was soaring around the skies and those nightmares were growing.

The nightmares of World III: from my journals

In the first week of the month of all these nightmares, a trio of people – all unconnected – messaged and emailed me with the details of their experiences. One of those was an alien abductee named Kenny. A resident of San Bernardino, California, Kenny had a trauma-filled dream of a nuclear attack on the United States on the night of August 7. In the nightmare, Kenny was relaxing, watching television, in a house in a small town near Lubbock, Texas – a city he has not visited; at least, not yet. Relaxation soon turned to absolute terror. A deep, thunderous rumbling noise suddenly filled the air. He raced to the front-door, only to see a huge radioactive cloud hanging in the distance – perhaps five or six miles away; maybe more.

Kenny was frozen to the spot, unable to move as the shock enveloped him that America had been hit by a devastating nuclear weapon. Then, as the blast from the detonation raced across the flat plains of West Texas, the sky turned dark and a massive wall of flame – perhaps two hundred feet high – destroyed everything in its wake. The last thing Kenny remembered before waking up in a frantic state, was the sight of another explosion, this one right on Lubbock itself. The war to outdo all wars had begun. Civilization, Kenny knew, would soon be over.

Not only that: Kenny, in one of his nightmares, had seen a *"huge black bird."*

There was also the story of Kimberly J. Her experience reached me just a couple of days after Kenny contacted me. Living in the heart of Chicago, Kimberly had heard of the growing sightings of the Mothman and, as an alien abductee herself, viewed the whole situation as scary and ominous. In her very own nightmare, Kimberly saw the destruction of Chicago by a nuclear weapon, with millions of people killed in seconds and the whole city destroyed. Most intriguing is the fact that Kimberly saw what she described as an approximately nine-foot-tall "bird-man" hovering over the radioactive remains and the terribly injured survivors of the initial blast. She got a feeling that the bird-man was "watching the end of us." It may well have been planning on doing just that.

Let's now turn to a good friend of mine who approached me about all this when it first began: Chris O'Brien. He's the author of a number of books, such as *Stalking the Herd*; *The Mysterious Valley*; and *Secrets of the Mysterious Valley*. Chris, very generously, said to me the following about all of this Armageddon-driven material:

Back in 2005 Grandfather Martin Gashweseoma, for many decades the 'Fire Clan Prophecy Tablet' holder, spent a week with Naia and I at our home in Sedona, AZ. We had met him 10 years prior and we had become friendly with the then 83 year old Traditional Elder. During one conversation about the predicted 'End of the Fourth World,' I asked him how the dreaded "War of the Gourd of Ashes'end." Not good; not good, in the slightest.

In 1989, Martin announced the start of the final conflict would begin within the year and it did with "Desert Storm." He said that North Korea would send fiery birds high in the sky to the US. I pressed him for further details suggesting maybe he meant China, and he said "No, Korea will be behind this attack, possibly w/ the help (or at the behest) of China." At the time Korea had no functioning nuclear weapons program and no ICBMs. As we all know, this has changed...Just thought I'd mention this!"

Another one who contacted me was a man named Stephen Polak. He told me something that absolutely chilled me. And, I can't blame him: 'As a Chicago resident myself who has recently had a dream of being consumed [by] an enormous wall of fire, I find all of this rather disquieting...' I couldn't disagree with Stephen.

MORE OF MY PAPERS: BEWARE OF THE FUTURE

On August 12, I received a Facebook message of a similar nature; this one from Jacob, an American who is now a resident of Mulhouse, France. In Jacob's dream, an emergency broadcast message appeared on his TV screen, warning people to take cover: the nukes were flying. And that was it: just a few, brief, seconds of mayhem in the dream-state. But, it was still an undeniably nightmarish night for Jacob.

It must be said, it's not at all impossible that at least *some* of this may have been due to the growing tensions between North Korea and the United States. On August 9, 2017, the U.K.'s *Independent* newspaper ran an article on the North Korea issue which stated, in part, that: "While it's unclear if North Korea can successfully target US cities like Denver *and Chicago* [italics mine] with a nuclear ICBM, it's similarly unknown if U.S. defense systems can strike it down - adding to American anxieties."

Curiously – or not - back in the 1970s, as a kid, I spent several holidays in Mulhouse. I can't figure out, at all, what that might mean. Maybe it means nothing, at all!"

A 2016-2017 PHENOMENON WON'T GO AWAY

One of the strangest of all the situations I've been in, began in 2016; although, I certainly didn't know it at the time. The key figure in this story? I'll tell you. It was Brad Steiger. Yes, *that* Brad Steiger. As many of you'll know, Brad was someone who was knowledgeable in many aspects of the supernatural, the para-normal, the cryptozoological, the conspiratorial, the ufological, the ghostly and much more.

It was one day when Brad and I were talking about the possi-bility of writing a book together. We had already written one book as a duo, *The Zombie Book.* So, working with Brad was certainly no problem, at all. There was, though, another thing: on one of the days when we were chatting, I said to Brad that he should really write a book on Mothman. Brad, of course, had realized the 50th anniversary of the Mothman phenomenon would be coming in the next year, 2017. It just might have been be a good time to write a book on John Keel's red-eyed monster. But, there was a sense of doom, Brad said.

First, Brad suggested to me I should take a look at his 1976 book, *Psychic City Chicago.* Brad also suggested that it might be a good thing if I were to write my own Mothman book. Admittedly, I *had* thought of the idea. Brad, though, had something else to say.

It went something like this: "Nick, read that book; you'll need it for next year [the 50th anniversary of the Mothman anniversary, of course]. I asked: "Why?"

Apparently, because Brad had been having horrible dreams of…*nuclear war*. Holy crap. And, he had been feeling he needed to look back to his 2011 book, *Real Monsters, Gruesome Critters, And Beasts From The Darkside*. Notably, Brad's book has more than a bit of Mothman-monster-material in its pages.

When, now, I look back to 2016, it makes me wonder how much more Brad knew: those nightmares, Mothman, those red eyes and the contents of Brad's *Psychic City Chicago* book [which I bought in quick time, I should say]. And, there was the matter of 2017 being a very dangerous time to live in. Somewhere in all of this, there was a handful of secrets still yet to come.

CHAPTER 21:

A WORLD WAR III COMING?

On the day of August 21, 2017, I received these fascinating – yet worrying - words from Jacqueline Bradley: "A few days ago I had a dream that several nuclear events occurred – in my dream. I remember the term 'thermonuclear.' There were several of these events popping up. Indeed, they appeared to be everywhere. Jacqueline said there were small versions of what we would ordinarily be aware of. No one seemed to be very perturbed by these and people were just walking around, occasionally looking around and watching these.

It was almost macabre.

Jacqueline continued with her story: "I was aware that if you were caught up in one [of these events] and died it killed off your soul or spirit, too. All this was happening in broad daylight on sunny days. The dream ended where I was in some kind of alley with an old fashioned dustbin nearby. Suddenly, I found myself 'sinking' or evaporating and woke up. I wasn't scared by the dream, just puzzled. I, too, connected it with the tensions in North Korea. I've also been watching *Twin Peaks* and connected it with that, but not sure why."

THE WORLD OF THE UFO CONTACTEE SOON SURFACED

Barely twenty-four hours later, Jill S. Pingleton got in touch with me: "As a paranormal investigator and student of metaphysics, I, like many, are concerned about the prophetic potential of so many having these dreams/visions. However, as a former MUFON Chief Investigator, I'm wondering if the people reporting these dreams and associations are Contactees?"

Jill made a very good point with her words: "My point is that Contactees frequently recount stories of viewing scenes of mass destruction placed in their mind's eye during encounters with ETs. I don't know if they are being given glimpses of the future. Or, only a possible time-line change. Like a wake-up call to Contactees. To get involved and speak out for the sake of humanity. Perhaps that's also the mission of the Mothman. I wonder if any of these dreams / visions were preceded by an abduction event, or if it's part of an on-going "download" that so many Contactees experience.

"I think much can be learned from studying the experiencers / witnesses. So many questions! Thank you for the articles and your insight into all these."

DID INDRID COLD COME BACK?

Back in early June of 2017, a man named Andy Berry had a horrible dream of being in a deserted version of London, England. The city was not destroyed or in flames. It was, said Andy, that the population had been "evacuated." It was an interesting phrase to use. Well, I say the city was deserted. It was, except for two things: one was the sight of "a massive, big black bird over [the Houses of] Parliament."

Then, as Andy walked the streets, trying to figure out what on Earth had happened, he had that feeling we all get from time to time; of someone watching them. He turned around to see a man in a black trench-coat right behind him. The man was pale, gaunt and – as Andy worded it – "he had a funny smile."

Andy's description of the "Creeper" sounded very much like a certain, sinister M.I.B.-like character in the saga of the Mothman story. You might already have thought who I meant. Yes: Indrid Cold. Andy, then, woke up with his heart pounding and his mouth dry, and relieved that it had just been a dream, after all. Or, was it something more than just a dream? A parallel London to the London that he lived in? Was it possible? Whatever the answers were, Andy said he would do his best to find all the answers. He never did get back to me. I'm not really surprised.

THE NUKE DREAMS GREW AND GREW

Over at the *Red Dirt Report* website, Andrew W. Griffin wrote an article titled "Riders on the storm (Strange days have tracked us down)." In his article, Andrew said: "Clearly we are entering very troubled waters. And it seems that the collective unconscious of humanity is clueing in that we are entering a perilous period in our history." Interestingly, Andrew added that in relation to Kenny's dream of a nuclear bomb exploding near Lubbock, Texas, it was "…not unlike my own dream that I wrote about on Jan. 26, 2017, which involved nuclear detonations near Joplin, Missouri." Andrew expanded further:

"We were in a car in the vicinity of Joplin, Missouri – something I noted in my mind in that it is on that nexus of high weirdness 37 degrees north and 94 degrees west (which I recently addressed here) – and nuclear explosions, followed by menacing mushroom clouds, are going off at various intervals…And yet as the nuclear blasts send radioactive debris through the town and infecting everything in its path, I seem to be the only one alarmed by what is happening around us. The whole experience has the feeling of a guided-tour through a park or historic site…"

By late August, I had received a total of twenty-seven dreams - of the destruction of Chicago and of other U.S. cities - via Facebook, my blog, and email. Of those twenty-seven, nineteen were from people in the United States, three from Canada, two from the U.K., two from Australia, and one from Mexico. Of the twenty-seven nightmares, twenty-three of them occurred in the previous three months. I continued with my statistics.

CHAPTER 22:

ELECTROMAGNETIC PULSE
TECHNOLOGY AND MOTHMAN

There is another aspect to all of this matter of Mothman and nuclear war. Over a time of eight weeks, no less than nine people contacted me after they had terrifying experiences in their sleep. In every one of the nightmares, the United States was destroyed by gigantic explosions, and across the whole U.S.: "Mushroom" blasts, of course. But, who initiated it all? No-one knew because all of the United States' military arsenal was flattened and unable to respond. None of the United States' nukes could be launched. Planes couldn't take to the sky. Cars and trucks were frozen. Laptops were dead. U.S. Military submarines sunk to the beds of the oceans, unable to help. All the electricity was lost just before the attacks. And there never would be any electric again.

Three of those eight people saw in their nightmares huge, black birds circling in a dust-filled atmosphere. There is, however, a very important question that has to be addressed: How could the United States have been flattened by Russia? Or, were the Chinese the culprits? North Korea? Maybe, they had all joined together to destroy the United States.

I realized immediately what had happened. There was only

one answer for all this. It was the science of electromagnetic Pulse (EMP) technology. EMP has the ability to totally paralyze technology of all kinds and across miles. Thankfully, those dreams were just that: dreams. But, in the real world, EMP weaponry can, indeed, bring down the most powerful technology to the ground. Were those EMP dreams really just dreams? I hope so.

THE U.S. GOVERNMENT GETS INVOLVED

Now, let's take a look at what the U.S. Government says about Electromagnetic Pulse technology. On September 6, 2022, the Department of Homeland Security (DHS) released this statement:

> Today, the Department of Homeland Security (DHS) released a report of operational approaches to protect the National Public Warning System from an electromagnetic pulse (EMP). The report is a collaborative effort between the DHS Science and Technology (S&T), the Federal Emergency Management Agency (FEMA) Integrated Public Alert and Warning System (IPAWS) Program, and the Cybersecurity & Infrastructure Security Agency (CISA). The report summarizes recommendations that federal, state, local agencies, and private sector critical infrastructure owners and operators can employ to protect against the effects of an EMP event.
>
> Electromagnetic pulses, whether caused by an intentional EMP attack or a naturally occurring geomagnetic disturbance from severe space weather, could disrupt critical infrastructure such as the electrical grid, communications equipment, water and wastewater systems, and

transportation modes," said Kathryn Coulter Mitchell, DHS Senior Official Performing the Duties of the Under Secretary for Science and Technology. "This could impact millions of people over large parts of the country. It is critical to protect against the potential damage an EMP event could cause.

The National Public Warning System ensures the President of the United States can communicate with Americans in the event of a national emergency. The FEMA IPAWS Program equips 77 private sector radio broadcast stations with EMP-protected backup trans-mitters, communications equipment, and power gener-ators that would enable the station to broadcast national emergency information to the public in the event of an EMP event.

These stations represent a key public-private sector partnership and serve as the primary sources for a national emergency broadcast during a catastrophic disaster, said Antwane Johnson, FEMA IPAWS Program Director. The stations are located across the country providing radio broadcast coverage to more than 90 percent of U.S. population.

As part of a broader DHS effort to ensure critical infrastructure and emergency response systems are pro-tected against EMPs, FEMA conducted high-altitude electromagnetic pulse (HEMP) testing on the NPWS equipment to evaluate its operational resiliency. The test-ing confirmed the effectiveness of protection for NPWS stations, showing they could withstand the effects of an EMP in accordance with military specifications.

Protecting critical assets from EMP is part of a larger DHS effort to assess and mitigate EMP risk in both the public and private sector, said Acting CISA Assistant Director Mona Harrington. CISA remains committed to working with our partners to implement requirements outlined in the Executive Order on Coordinating National Resilience to Electromagnetic Pulses, which strengthens our nation's preparedness from EMP.

The best practices and design principles noted in the Electromagnetic Pulse Shielding Mitigations report can be implemented by critical infrastructure owners and operators who seek to secure their assets against EMP in a similar manner to the NPWS equipment.

It's not just the Department of Homeland Security that is concerned about EMP technology. The Division of Environmental Health, Office of Radiation Protection is worried, too. They *should* be worried. We *all* should. Back to the U.S. government:

The most important mechanism for Electromagnetic Pulse (EMP) production from a nuclear detonation is the ionization of air molecules by gamma rays generated from the explosion. These gamma rays ionize the air molecules by interacting with the air molecules to produce positive ions and recoil electrons called Compton electrons. This pulse of energy, which produces a powerful electromagnetic field, particularly within the
vicinity of the weapon burst, is called an electromagnetic pulse. EMP can also be produced from non-nuclear sources, such as electromagnetic bombs, or E-bombs.

High-altitude nuclear detonations and electromagnetic bombs can generate EMP that has the potential to damage or destroy electronic devices over widespread areas. Electric power systems would also be at risk from surges produced by such weapons. However, the EMP from a kiloton-range surface nuclear explosion would not be expected to produce serious damage outside the radius of severe destruction from blast. A 1.4 Megaton bomb launched about 250 miles above Kansas would destroy most of the electronics that were not protected in the entire Continental United States. During the brief return to atmospheric testing in 1962, a 1.4 megaton nuclear weapon was detonated over Johnston Island at an altitude of about 250 miles. The effects of EMP were observed in Hawaii, 800 miles east of the detonation. Streetlights and fuses failed on Oahu and telephone service was disrupted on the Island of Kauai.

Now, we know the potential, sheer, horrific power of EMP technology. And, the ability to use it as weaponry across masses of land. Particularly nuclear weapons. There are three more things that need to be remembered about this: namely, (A) Whitley Strieber; (B) his 1984 book, *Warday*; and (C) the Mothman-type creature that we heard of in the pages of *Warday*. Was Strieber given a look – or, rather, a glance - at the future? Did those nine people, who approached me about a destroyed United States, have a glance of a real, future world? A world in which EMP was used and with no looking back, at all. And no civilization left. *Ever.*

CHAPTER 23:

FROM 1963 TO NOW

It wouldn't surprise me if the story I'm about to share with you, now, really resonates. It began in the 1960s, but resurfaced just a few years ago. Keel mentioned the story, very briefly, in *The Mothman Prophecies*, but, there was much more to things than that, as you'll soon see. The whole thing went down in November 1963 and has more than a few parallels with the Mothman enigma. But, the really important part of the story is this: certain, new portions of the story have since surfaced and have barely been seen before. So, that's the reason why we're going to take a trip to Hythe, Kent, England; a town that has Saxon and Norman connections. In other words, it's a very old area! As for the Kent monster, let's get right to it.

The whole thing fascinated me when the latter day part of the story opened up, because of the ways in which the Hythe monster paralleled the terror that came down on Point Pleasant. No wonder I pursued the story.

AN AMERICAN MOTHMAN AND A U.K. MOTHMAN?

Midway through November 1963 (very close to when President John F. Kennedy was killed in downtown Dallas, Texas), one of the most chilling and eerie of all monster encounters on record occurred in the dark and shadowy environment of Sandling Park, Hythe, Kent, England. It was an encounter that, in terms of the description of the creature, provokes Mothman-style imagery – even though the latter, famous creature did not hit the major headlines in and around Point Pleasant, West Virginia until the mid-1960s onwards. Although Sandling Park was certainly shrouded in overwhelming darkness at the time of the beastly event, it was hardly the sort of place where one would expect to encounter nothing less than a fully-fledged monster. Amazingly, however, and according to a group of terrified witnesses, that is exactly what happened.

John Flaxton, age seventeen on the night that all hell broke loose, was accompanied by three friends, including eighteen-year old Mervyn Hutchinson. As they walked by the park – after returning from a local Friday night dance – the group of friends became aware of a bright object moving overhead, which they, at first, took to be nothing stranger than a star. How very wrong they turned out to be.

The teenagers were amazed, and more than a bit scared, by the object's presence, as they watched it hover and then drop out of sight behind a group of trees. The boys decided to leave the area with haste, but the light soon loomed into view again. *It hovered around ten feet from the ground* [italics mine], and at an approximate distance of two hundred feet, it went out of sight.

"It was a bright and gold oval," one of the boys reported. "And when *we* moved, *it* moved. When *we* stopped, *it* stopped." That was not necessarily a good sign!

Suddenly, the boys heard the snapping of twigs from a nearby thicket. And, out from the wooded area shuffled a creature of horrendous appearance. "It was the size of a human," said Mervyn Hutchinson, but the words to come would be notable: "*It didn't seem to have any head. There were wings on its back, like bat wings* [italics mine]." The group fled, perhaps understandably not wanting to hang around and see what developed next.

Matters didn't end there, however. Five nights later, Keith Croucher saw an unusual object floating across a nearby soccer field. Forty-eight-hours after that, a man named John McGoldrick, accompanied by a friend, checked out the location and stumbled upon unusual impressions in the ground, which gave every indication that something solid and significant had landed there.

Neil Arnold, a researcher of paranormal and monstrous phenomena, who lives in the English county of Kent, had this to say about the matter: "Local UFO experts believed that the case was nothing more than a misinterpretation of natural phenomena. But, Flaxton recalled: 'I felt cold all over.'"

And, as Arnold also noted: "Three giant footprints were also found in the vicinity which were said to have measured two-feet long and nine inches across. On 11 December, various newspaper reporters accompanied McGoldrick to the area and found that the woods were illuminated by an eerie, glowing light. No-one investigated any further and the case faded as mysteriously as it had emerged."

Things stayed to that situation until 2017; the 50th anniversary of the appearances of the Mothman. That date of 2017 keeps coming around. I'm sure you've noticed that.

DEVELOPMENTS AND SIMILARITIES

There's no doubt that the person who really opened this story in 2017 was Allison Jornlin, a definitive sleuth-meets-bulldog and then morphs into one. It's very important to know that Allison has a fascination for the Mothman mystery and that's what caused her to take a look at this new material that came to the surface.

It was because of Allison's deep digging that some new, fascinating material came along. Interestingly, it all happened in a "Lovers Lane" area. We'll get to the "Lovers Lane" phenomenon soon.

While looking for more information on the Hythe case, Allison found a copy of an old newspaper: it was the December 1, 1963 edition of Australia's *Sydney Morning Herald*. It contained something incredible: the newly-found, years-old, article. It was titled "*Ghost Haunts Lovers' Lane*." Allison had more to say. The reporter who pursued the case in the first place wrote these intriguing words: "A local rector is tracking down a reported black magic circle that has been blamed for the 'terror.'" As for the rector, his official title was the Reverend E. Stanton, of Saltwood. There was still more to come.

THE STORY GROWS AND GROWS

The nearby journalists were fired up. No wonder! Of course they were. What else? One of the journalists penned these words: "The ghost is said to be of William Tournay Tournay [yes, he had two names the same], a rich, eccentric landowner who was buried 60 years ago on an island in the middle of a lake at Saltwood, near Hythe village, in Kent."

Matters were still rolling, as the reverend made clear: "Several young people in the village have come to see me saying they have seen the ghost. There are rumors that a black magic circle meets in a secret hideout in the village and that they are responsible. I have no proof yet that they are working in Saltwood, but I'm determined to get to the bottom of this business because it's disrupting village life."

All of this seemed to be expanding by the hour. Maybe by the minute. As the sadly now-deceased UFO-seeker Robbie Graham wrote to the media: "Allison Jornlin has been investigating hauntings and other strange phenomena for more than 20 years and is the recipient of the 2016 Wisconsin Researcher of the Year Award from the Milwaukee Paranormal Conference. Allison was inspired by Chicago's Richard Crowe, who kick-started U.S. ghost tourism in 1973, and she developed Milwaukee's first haunted history tour in 2008." Impressive.

"Since then, she has led numerous haunted history tours and presented talks on a variety of Fortean topics; poltergeists, UFOs, cryptids, and demonic possession."

CHAPTER 24:

A FLYING WOMAN IN VIETNAM
AND SOLDIER OF FORTUNE

One of the strangest, and undoubtedly, creepiest of all encounters with a winged creature occurred at the height of the Vietnam War, and specifically in Da Nang, Vietnam – *but, it has a modern day aspect, as you will see.* It was in August 1969 that a man named Earl Morrison, along with several comrades, had the shock of his life. It was, very appropriately, in the dead of night when the menacing event occurred – and as the men were on guard-duty, keeping a careful look out for the Vietcong. Everything was quiet and normal until around 1:30 a.m. That's when the atmosphere changed, and an eerie form made its presence known to the shocked men of the US 1st Division Marine Corps.

Despite being somewhat reluctant to speak out publicly, Morrison eventually changed his mind and, by 1972, was comfortable about discussing the incident, even if he wasn't comfortable with what he encountered. His story makes for incredible reading:

"We saw what looked like wings, like a bats, only it was gigantic compared to what a regular bat would be. After it got close enough so we could see what it was, it looked like a woman. A naked woman. She was black. Her skin was black, her body was black, the wings were back; everything was black. But it glowed. It glowed in the night, kind of greenish cast to it. She started going over us, and we still didn't hear anything. She was right above us, and when she got over the top of our heads she was maybe 6 or 7 feet up. We watched her go straight over the top of us, and she still didn't make any noise flapping her wings.

She blotted out the moon once – that's how close she was to us. And dark – looked like pitch black then, but we could still define her because she just glowed. Real bright like. And she started going past us straight towards our encampment. As we watched her – she had got about 10 feet or so away from us – we started hearing her wings flap. And it sounded, you know, like regular wings flapping. And she just started flying off and we watched her for quite a while."

One of those who took a great deal of interest in the story of the flying woman of Da Nang was a UFO researcher named Don Worley. His personal interview with Morrison revealed additional data, such as the fact that the woman's hair was black and straight, that the wings may have had a slight furry quality to them, that she "rippled" as she flew by, that she appeared to lack bones in her body, and that her wings seemed to be directly "molded" to her hands and arms.

The investigators, Janet and Colin Bord, say of this particularly odd case: "Usually our reports of winged figures describe them as 'men,' but without any indication whether features are seen which tell the witness definitely that it is a man. In view of this we suspect that so-called 'birdmen' should strictly be termed 'bird people' or 'bird persons,' and that no sex attribution can honestly be made."

FROM VIETNAM TO A BIZARRE THEORY

Now, to something that's absolutely wild and that just *might* be tied to the story directly above. That is, if you have a *really* crazy imagination. On January 9, 2014, the John Keel website stated the following: "Mark Pilkington [a journalist and author who specializes in weird things] has alerted me to the fact that the current issue of *Soldier of Fortune* magazine (Feb. '14) contains an article entitled 'UFO Mystery Solved: "Mothmen' Were Actually Green Berets.'"

The writer, Harold Hutchison, claims that special operations forces near Point Pleasant were testing high-altitude, low-opening (HALO) parachuting for use in Vietnam; and that the jumpers used luminous paint to be seen during the tests. And this, he says, explains the Mothman sightings."

The people at the *Haunted Librarian* website weren't impressed: "While Hutchison's theory is interesting and places a patriotic spin on Mothman, a truly Americana urban legend, it doesn't make sense. So, no, Mothman was not a wayward Green Beret."

CHAPTER 25:

IT'S NOT ONLY MOTHMAN THAT'S SINISTER AND PARANORMAL IN POINT PLEASANT

MY NOTES ON THESE CREEPY KIDS

There can be no doubt that one of the creepiest phenomena to have surfaced in the last two decades is that of what have become infamously known as the Black-Eyed Children. It would be overly simplistic to suggest they are merely the offspring of the Men in Black and the Women in Black. Admittedly, though, there are deep similarities. And, also like the MIB and the WIB, the BEC are definitive drainers of energy. Now, let's first take a look at how, and under what specific circumstances, the Black-Eyed Children came to prominence. Then, we'll get to the matter of the Black Eyed Children at...Point Pleasant. If Mothman isn't enough.

Although, today, we have people who claim to have seen the BEC in the period from the 1930s to the present day, the very first reported case didn't surface until January

1998. The location was the Lone Star State, specifically the city of Abilene. The story revolves around a man named Brian Bethel, a journalist who works for the *Abilene Reporter News*. It was late one night when Bethel's life was changed and he came to realize that there are dangerous, supernatural entities in our midst.

It was close to 10:00 p.m. when Bethel had the kind of close encounter that one never, ever forgets. He had pulled up at a mall not too far from his home, to deposit a check in a mail-box. All was quiet and dark. Bethel, using the lights of the mall to illuminate the interior of his vehicle, was writing the check when he was rudely interrupted. He jumped with surprise at the sight of a couple of kids who were standing next to the car, on the driver's side. But, there was something about these kids that rang alarm bells in Bethel's head. In fact, as Bethel would imminently learn, things were wrong in the extreme.

Danger by night

Bethel stared at the pair and couldn't fail to see just how incredibly pale the face of one of the boys was. The other had what Bethel described as olive-colored skin. Both boys were around ten to fourteen years of age, Bethel estimated, and both were dressed in pullovers. Only one of the two boys spoke – he claimed that they wanted to see a movie, *Mortal Kombat*, at the local cinema. But, there was a problem: they had left their money at home. Could Bethel take them to their homes to get some cash? Bethel near-instantly realized that this whole situation had an air of dark and disturbing theater about it. There was an undeniably unsettling agenda at work, and it had absolutely zero to do with movies.

Bethel awkwardly hemmed and hawed for a few moments, something which caused the talkative boy to become ever more insistent that Bethel let them in the car. Then, things became downright eerie and chilling: Bethel found himself almost mind-manipulated, to the point where, to his horror, he could see that his hand was heading to the driver's-side door – *with the intent of opening it, but without his control.* Bethel, fortunately, broke the enchanting spell and didn't open the door, after all. This clearly incensed the talkative boy, who amped up the pleas to allow them into Bethel's car. It was then, for the first time, that Bethel finally got a good look at their eyes. In his own words - referenced in *Pararational's* May 16, 2013 article titled "Brian Bethel – The Black Eyed Kids" – Bethel stated: "They were coal black. No pupil. No iris."

The two boys realized that, by now, they were losing the battle to be permitted to get into Bethel's car. On this very point, Bethel himself said that the boy who did all of the talking "wore a mask of anger."

The boy, now displaying a look on his face which was part-frustration and part-anger, almost shouted: "We can't come in unless you tell us it's okay. Let us in!" Bethel, terrified, did nothing of the sort. What he *did* do was to slam the car into reverse and head for home, completely panicked by the whole thing. Oddly, as he drove away, Bethel looked back, only to see that the boys were nowhere in sight. In what was clearly and impossibly quick time, they had vanished.

And, thus was quickly born a legend. It's a legend that shows no signs of stopping. It's only getting worse.

Point Pleasant has yet another mystery...a sinister one

The West Virginia city of Point Pleasant is inextricably linked to the legend of the red-eyed Mothman, that flying fiend which terrorized the people of Point Pleasant from late 1966 to December 1967. In 2012, though, it was *black* eyes – rather than *red* eyes – which caused so much terror for one woman, who we'll call "Marie." Although Marie's BEC encounter occurred in 2012, she did not speak about it until two years later. She was in her mid-twenties when she had an encounter she was destined to never, ever forget. There is no doubt that the fear in Marie's face was as clear as it was obvious when she related the facts to me at the 2014 Mothman Festival - which is held in Point Pleasant every September, and which attracts people in their thousands.

From a face-to-face interview with Marie

Marie worked irregular hours in her job. As a result, on a Saturday night, shortly after 11:00 p.m., she was stretched out on her couch, in front of the TV, after a ten-hour-long stint at work. She had got herself a pizza and a couple of cans of beer. All was good. For a while.

Marie practically flew off the couch with fear as there was a loud knock on the front door of her second-floor apartment. She thought: who the hell could that be at this time of night? It was a very good question. Marie carefully crept silently to the door and looked through the spy-hole, her breathing already slightly labored. There were two boys, staring back at her, and both wearing black hoodies. She asked if they were okay. No reply. That wasn't a good sign: Marie put the chain on the door and then opened it the couple of inches that the chain would allow. Two things immediately struck Marie – and filled her with fear: their skin was as white as a sheet of paper. One of them, in a monotone and blank fashion, demanded "food."

Not surprisingly, Marie slammed the door, and ran to the furthest wall in the living room. Her mind was in a whirlwind of confusion and fear. After a few minutes, she again crept to the door and looked through the spyhole: the boys were still there. Most disturbing of all, the pair clearly reacted when Marie looked at them – even though she had done so in complete silence. Then, something even more terrifying happened: the pair of "children," suddenly shimmered – like a "heatwave," said Marie – and transformed into a pair of bipedal, lizard-like monsters. In seconds, they were swallowed up by a sudden, black nothingness outside the door and were gone. It's hardly surprising that when she was satisfied that all was okay, Marie fled her apartment and went to stay with her mother for the next three days, who lived in nearby Ohio.

Now, to *another* bizarre encounter from Point Pleasant:

Anna is a thirty-five-year-old resident of none other than Point Pleasant, West Virginia – the infamous locale where, in 1966, the notorious, blazing-eyed Mothman first surfaced, and which was made legendary in John Keel's classic book, *The Mothman Prophecies*. As Anna revealed to me when I was at Point Pleasant in 2014 - to speak at the annual Mothman Festival – back in October 2012 she had a strange and frightening encounter with a pair of Black-Eyed Children, late one Saturday night. Anna, a shift-worker at a local factory, was spending her night relaxing and watching television, after a hard day of work. Sometime around 11:10 p.m., there was a knock at the door. Do I need to tell you who had just arrived?

Anna warily went to the door, and peered through the spyhole. She couldn't fail but to see the two boys, standing next to each other, and both wearing the familiar black hoodies. She shouted through the door, asking what they wanted. When she got no answer, Anna put the chain on the door and opened it. When Anna saw the boys, she was frozen with terror: both had the ubiquitous black eyes, and both had skin the color of milk. "We need food," said one, in an almost robotic fashion, while looking at his feet. Oddly, his companion was also steadfastly looking down. With hindsight, Anna felt that their stances reflected their attempts to try and prevent her from seeing their strange eyes. If so, it was an attempt that failed spectacularly.

Anna slammed the door, shaking with fear as she did so. For a few minutes she retreated to the furthest part of the living room. When, however, there was no further knock at the door, she made a tentative move. Plucking up all her courage, Anna peered once again through the spyhole: the two boys were still there. Most disturbing of all, although Anna practically tiptoed towards the door and did not touch it as she reached it, she said that the BECs clearly reacted as she looked at them, as if they were able to sense she was just behind the other side of the door.

As Anna continued to stare at them – locked into a state of terror – something almost unimaginable happened: an eerie green glow surrounded the boys and, in seconds, they were replaced by a pair of what Anna described as large, upright lizards. The monstrous pair stood around eight feet tall, were completely naked, and had long, protruding jaws filled with razor-sharp teeth. They did nothing but stand there, for around twenty seconds or so, after which, Anna explained, the outside porch was enveloped in blackness and they vanished from view. Her first thought was to call the local police. But, she felt – almost certainly correctly – that filing such an incident with law-enforcement officials would very likely cause her even more problems. Instead, she quickly packed a bag, carefully opened the door, raced to her car, and spent the next three days staying at her mother's place, just over the Ohio River. It was the end of a shocking and unforgettable incident.

CHAPTER 26:

HEADING TO MOTHMAN TERRITORY

Although I've been to Point Pleasant on many occasions – usually to give lectures at the yearly festival in town - my trip to the city in 2017 was more like a road-trip, something I love. There was several of us: me, Lyle Blackburn, Ken Gerhard and several friends. They are devotees of road-trips, too. The drive there (and back) is *beyond* long; but it's always worth it. So, we filled our vehicle with all the things we needed and hit the road. We rolled into town – slightly blearily-eyed and frazzled from a lack of sleep – around 5:00 p.m., checked into our motel, and then, as darkness fell, headed out to a local pizza eatery. There were about twenty of us there, including John and Tim Frick, who I first met at the September 2014 Mothman gig. If you don't know the Frick brothers, you should.

Not only do the brothers know just about everything when it comes to Mothman history, they also know the town itself very well. And, particularly, the many and varied landmarks which are linked to the story of Mothman. Around 8:00 p.m., they took us –with other friends – to the old, so-called TNT area, which has played such an integral role in the Mothman saga. As we left the pizza place, a full-blown convoy of vehicles followed Tim and

John, as we traveled along small, winding, tree-shrouded, roads to the scene of the old action. No surprise, there was an atmosphere of excitement and anticipation in the increasingly chilly air.

For those who may not know, the TNT area's official title is the McClintic Wildlife Management Area. It's situated around five miles north of the town of Point Pleasant and runs to more than 3,500 acres. At the height of the Second World War, a TNT processing plant was established in the area, with the volatile chemicals used to create it stored in a series of concrete, igloo-like buildings.

It was the work of around 3,500 U.S. Army personnel and, at the time, was known as the West Virginia Ordnance Works. Today, the plant is no more. The only things left now are the crumbling foundations and a couple of sturdy, metal, perimeter-gates and a rusted metal fence. During daylight, it's an inviting and picturesque area, filled with densely-packed trees, a plethora of wildlife – such as deer, raccoons and beavers – and numerous ponds, pools and small lakes. After dark, however, things are very different. The atmosphere of menace, which was so present back in the sixties, is *still* there – utterly refusing to relinquish its icy grip on the people of Point Pleasant. And, the TNT locale is gone.

Having checked out what was left of the old plant, we all followed John and Tim to a specific stretch of heavily wooded ground, parked our vehicles, and were given an excellent and atmospheric tour of the igloos and their surroundings. I have to say the whole thing reminded me of something straight out of *The Walking Dead*: a ruined, overgrown environment, a once bustling area now utterly dead and abandoned, and an almost apocalyptic air that one could practically cut with a knife. The military was nowhere in sight, and the igloos were decaying, covered in foliage, and splattered with graffiti, both old and new.

Me and a good friend, Denise, broke off from the main group and checked out some of the igloos, which was a profoundly memorable experience: the size and shape of the igloos cause a person's voice to echo loudly and very oddly within their dark confines. Plus, we felt a deep sense of malignancy in the old buildings – a sense which was as immediate as it was long-lasting. You could almost taste the menace, if such a thing were possible.

Notably, there was some evidence that supernatural rites and rituals had been undertaken in some of the igloos, which I found most intriguing. It was near these very same igloos that so many of the Mothman sightings occurred in 1966 and 1967 – involving, it should be noted, witnesses who soon found themselves in the cold clutches of the Men in Black. Denise and I walked around, in near-darkness, for a couple of hours, with little more than the bright Moon for illumination, taking in the atmosphere and imagining what it must have been like decades ago earlier.

A few scurrying animals and the cries of a handful of geese flying overhead were pretty much the only things that convinced us we hadn't entered some strange portal – a doorway to an unsettling, dead world. After a while, we caught up with the rest of the gang. We hit the darkness-filled roads and headed back to our motels. It had been a cool night of high-strangeness.

Two days later we were on the road again, heading back to our homes. It was another great weekend and more stories told. And, of course, there was that memorable time spent with Susan Sheppard.

CHAPTER 27:

A FOREST AND A FLYING MONSTER

This particular story fell into my hands a few years ago and – from my perspective – it's a fascinating one. It's a story that I couldn't release for a long time; hence why I'm sharing it with you now. My notes (directly below) are now in the hands of the family that shared the papers with me:

Needwood Forest - of the county of Staffordshire, England - was a chase, or a royal forest, that was given to Henry III's son, Edmund Crouchback, the 1st Earl of Lancaster, in 1266, and was owned by the Duchy of Lancaster until it passed into the possession of Henry IV. In the 1770s, Francis Noel Clarke Mundy published a collection of poetry called *Needwood Forest* which contained his own poem of the same name, one regarded as "one of the most beautiful local poems. And much the same was said about the forest – which was an undeniably enchanting locale, filled with magic, myths and ancient lore, as forests so curiously often are.

Today, however, things are sadly very different, and most of the ancient woodland is now, tragically, gone:

presently, the area is comprised of twenty farms, on which dairy farming is the principal enterprise; and less than 500 acres of woodland now remain. Some parts of the forest are still open to the public, including Jackson Bank: a mature, mixed 80-acre area of woodland which can be found at Hoar Cross near Burton upon Trent and which is owned by the Duchy of Lancaster.

And then there is Bagot's Wood near Abbots Bromley, which claims to be the largest remaining part of Needwood Forest, and which takes its name from the Bagot family, seated for centuries at Staffordshire's Blithfield Hall. Situated some nine miles east of Stafford and 5 miles north of Rugeley, the Hall, has been the home of the Bagot family since the late 14th century; while the present house is mainly Elizabethan, with a Gothic façade added in the 1820s to a design probably by John Buckler.

In 1945 the Hall, then in a neglected and dilapidated state, was sold by Gerald Bagot, (the 5th Baron Bagot) together with its 650-acre estate to the South Staffordshire Waterworks Company, whose intention was to build a reservoir, and which was completed in 1953. The 5th Baron died in 1946, having sold many of the contents of the house. His successor and cousin, Caryl Bagot, repurchased the property and 30 acres of land from the water company and began an extensive program of both renovation and restoration.

The 6th Baron died in 1961 and bequeathed the property to his widow: Nancy, Lady Bagot. In 1986, the Hall was divided into four separate houses, the main part of which incorporates the Great Hall and is owned by the

Bagot Jewitt Trust. Lady Bagot and the Bagot Jewitt family remain in residence.

And, it is against this backdrop of ancient woodland and historic and huge old halls that something decidedly strange occurred back in the summer of 1937, when Alfred Tipton was but a ten-year-old boy. And like most adventurous kids, young Alfred enjoyed playing near Blithfield Hall, and in the Bagot's Wood, with his friends: on weekends and during the seemingly-never-ending school-holidays. And, it was during the summer holidays of 1937 that something strange and monstrous was seen in that small, yet eerie, area of old woodland.

According to Tipton, on one particular morning he and four of his friends had been playing in the woods for several hours and were taking a break, sitting on the warm, dry grass, and soaking in the sun. Suddenly, says Tipton, they heard a shrill screeching sound that was coming from the trees directly above them. As they craned their necks to look directly upwards, the five pals were horrified by the sight of a large, black beast sitting on its haunches in one particularly tall and very old tree, and "shaking the branch up and down with its claws tightened around it." But this was no mere large bird, however.

Tipton says that "it reminded me of a devil: I still don't forget things and it's what I say it looked like." He adds that the creature peered down at the five of them for a few moments and then suddenly opened up its large and shiny wings, which were easily a combined twelve-feet across, and took to the skies in a fashion that could be accurately described as part-flying and part-gliding, before being forever lost to sight after perhaps 15 or 20 seconds or so.

Significantly, when shown various pictures, photographs and drawings of a wide variety of large-winged creatures that either still roam our skies or did so in the past, the one that Tipton said most resembled the creature he and his mates saw was a pterodactyl. Of course, the pterodactyl is long extinct; however, Tipton is adamant that the beast the boys encountered was extremely similar to the legendary winged monster of the distant past.

Were the boys merely spooked and confused by their sighting of a large, exotic bird – albeit one of a conventional nature and origin, and perhaps even a circus- or zoo-escapee? Or, was some hideous winged-thing really haunting Bagot's Wood on that fateful, long-gone morning back in 1937? Sadly, probably neither we nor Alfred Tipton will ever know the answers to those thought-provoking and controversial questions.

CHAPTER 28:

A GLOWING HORROR IN HOUSTON

There's no doubt the story of what became known as the Houston Batman is a fascinating one. This critter was possibly the closest to Mothman when it comes to appearances. It all went down in the early 1950s and created terror and mayhem for a while in the area. In 2022, I decided to take a drive down to Houston and find the area where the monster was seen back in 1953. Sadly, the landscape of today is not what it was back then. In other words, the buildings near to where the creature was seen in 1953 are long gone: "Knocked down to the ground" is a better phrase. At least I managed to get the full story and save it. Here it is:

Certainly, one of the most bizarre of all the many and varied strange beings that haunts the lore and legend of Texas is that which became known, albeit very briefly, as the Houston Batman. The most famous encounter with the beast took place during the early morning hours of June 18, 1953. Given the fact that it was a hot and restless night, twenty three year old housewife Hilda Walker, and her neighbors, fourteen year old Judy Meyer and thirty three year old tool plant inspector Howard Phillips, were sitting on the porch of Walker's home, located at 118 East Third Street in the city of Houston.

Walker stated of what happened next: "…twenty five feet away I saw a huge shadow across the lawn. I thought at first it was the magnified reflection of a big moth caught in the nearby street light. Then the shadow seemed to bounce upward into a pecan tree. We all looked up. That's when we saw it."

She went on to describe the entity as being essentially man like in shape, sporting a pair of bat style wings, dressed in a black, tight-fitting outfit, and surrounded by an eerie, glowing haze. The trio all confirmed that the monstrous form stood about six and a half feet tall and also agreed that the strange glow engulfing him was yellow in color. The Batman vanished when the light slowly faded out and right about the time that Meyer issued an ear-splitting scream.

Mrs. Walker also recalled the following: "Immediately afterwards, we heard a loud swoosh over the house tops across the street. It was like the white flash of a torpedo-shaped object… I've heard so much about flying saucer stories and I thought all those people telling the stories were crazy, but now I don't know what to believe. I may be nuts, but I saw it, whatever it was… I sat there stupefied. I was amazed."

Meyer added to the newspaper that: "I saw it, and nobody can say I didn't."

Phillips, meanwhile, was candid in stating the following: "I can hardly believe it. But I saw it… we looked across the street and saw a flash of light rise from another tree and take off like a jet." For her part, Walker reported the incident to local police the following morning.

As a former resident of Houston, monster-hunter Ken Gerhard made valiant attempts to locate the address on East Third Street where the event took place and discovered that it is no longer in existence. It has seemingly been overtaken by the expansion of the nearby Interstate 10. Strangely, and perhaps even appropriately, the location has apparently vanished into the void – much like the Batman did, for a while at least.

Several years after he first heard about the exploits of the Batman, a close friend of Gerhard told him about the experience of a number of employees at Houston's Bellaire Theater, who claimed to have seen a gigantic, helmeted man, crouched down and attempting to hide on the roof of a downtown city building late one night during the 1990s.

Perhaps, in view of this latter day development, we should seriously consider the possibility that the Houston Batman made a return appearance. Or, maybe, it never went away at all. Instead, possibly, it has been lurking deep within the shadows of Houston, Texas for more than half a century, carefully biding its time, and only surfacing after the sun has set, and when overwhelming darkness dominates the sprawling metropolis.

CHAPTER 29:

BATSQUATCH: WHAT A NAME!

Practically everyone has heard of Bigfoot and Mothman. Along with the likes of the Loch Ness Monster and the Abominable Snowman, they are two of the world's most famous monsters. But, what do you get when you combine the aforementioned Bigfoot and Mothman? Well, what you get is Batsquatch: a terrifying, malevolent, hair-covered humanoid that sports a pair of huge, gargoyle-like wings. My own words:

"A curious semi-gliding, semi-flying fashion"

It was a diabolical beast encountered by a young man on the night of Saturday, April 16, 1994. The location was southeast of Buckley, Washington State, and with Mount Rainier in the background. Interestingly, Mount Rainier has another strange and now-famous aerial mystery attached to it: it was over the mountain, on June 24, 1947, that a pilot named Kenneth Arnold encountered a squadron of strange, flying vehicles that, when the media got hold of the story, became famously known as flying saucers. Meanwhile, however, back to 1994.

The man who became the unfortunate witness to the terrible beast was Brian Canfield, who, at the time in question, was driving his truck to Camp One, a settlement in the area, and which is situated near Lake Kapowsin. All was normal until Canfield's headlights began to fade. That was bad enough. But, in mere moments, his engine completely quit and his vehicle silently coasted to a stop at the side of the road. All thoughts of what he should do, on a lonely stretch of Washington State road at around 9:30 p.m., went totally out of the window when an infernal monstrosity loomed into view.

Canfield could only look on, terror-stricken, as a large, dark-colored humanoid descended from the black skies. It did so in a curious semi-gliding, semi-flying fashion, finally coming to rest right in front of his vehicle. Canfield was unable to move, such was his level of terror. All he could do was grip the steering wheel and stare in stark terror at the beast before him.

It was a shocking sight, to say the least. The winged, hair-covered monster was around nine feet in height and, as Canfield could now see, those wings spanned the entire road. It was at this point, despite his terror, that Canfield finally got a good look at the creature. Its fur was actually a dark blue, rather than the assumed black or brown. Its eyes shone yellow, and its white fangs protruded menacingly from its werewolf-like visage. For at least a couple of minutes, both man and monster confronted each other, neither making any kind of move. That is, until the creature, without warning, flapped its wings powerfully and violently and took to the skies.

Perhaps demonstrating the creature's supernatural powers, when the beast vanished Canfield's vehicle returned to normal: both its headlights and engine worked perfectly. Canfield raced back to the home he shared with his parents, charged into the house, and spluttered and gasped his way through his astounding story of what happened. Canfield's father, clearly realizing this was no prank, decided that the best thing they could do would be to get back out there and try and figure things out – as in right now. Perhaps luckily for both of them, Batsquatch – an undeniably memorable name, one which was name coined by one of Canfield's friends – was nowhere to be seen. And, so far as can be determined, it has never been seen again. Unless, that is, you know better.

CHAPTER 30:

"THEY LIVE IN THE SKY"

Make mention of UFOs and it will likely conjure up imagery of flying saucers and diminutive, black-eyed, large headed ETs, and alien abductions. At least some UFOs, however, may have absolutely nothing whatsoever to do with visitors from far away solar-systems and galaxies. Welcome to the world of a man named Trevor James Constable, who died in 2018, and who also had a connection to flying monsters:

> Having investigated the UFO phenomenon extensively, Constable penned two books on the subject. *They Live in the Sky* was published in 1958 and *Sky Creatures* followed two decades later. In deeply studying the UFO phenomenon, Constable came to a fascinating conclusion concerning what he believed to be the truth of the mystery surrounding flying saucers.
>
> Constable's conclusion was that UFOs are not nuts-and-bolts craft from distant worlds, but living creatures that inhabit the highest levels of the Earth's atmosphere. While many UFO investigators scoffed at Constable's undeniably unique ideas, none could deny that his theory

was well thought out. Describing them as "critters," Constable believed the creatures to be unicellular and amoeba-like, but having metallic-like outer-shells, which gave them their flying saucer-style appearances. He also believed they varied in size from extremely small to lengths approaching half a mile – which, admittedly accords with what UFO witnesses tell us: the assumed alien craft that people have reported do indeed vary from a few inches to massive, so-called "mother-ships."

If the skies of our planet *are* constantly populated by an untold number of airborne critters, then why don't we see them for what they really are – and on a regular basis? Constable had a notable and engaging theory for this, too: he believed the aerial things reflect infra-red light, which is not visible to the naked, human eye. However, Constable also believed the critters can change color, something which explains why they are occasionally seen, and sometimes quite out of the blue. It's not a case that they are here one minute and gone the next. For Constable, that was only how it appears. They're always here, in massive numbers; we're just not physically able to see them in their natural state. Constable also concluded that this theory explained why some UFO witnesses had photographed UFOs, but had not seen anything out of the ordinary when they took the picture. In other words, when it comes to Constable's sky-critters, the camera can see what the human eye cannot.

Constable believed that even though the sky-beasts possessed formidable powers that allowed them to remain out of sight – for the most part – they could be seen and photographed if one specifically used an infrared cine-film and a suitable filter. Constable even put his theories into practice – in the heart of the Mojave Desert. He claimed to have had considerable success in California's Lucerne Valley. Constable did not shy away from publishing his photos, which continue to provoke a great deal of debate – and, at times, unbridled fury – amongst the UFO faithful. It's important to note, however, that Constable's claims did not stand alone.

In May 1977, a UFO investigator named Richard Toronto – who had developed a fascination for Constable's theories – decided to try and replicate Constable's photos, also in the Mojave Desert. He claimed considerable success. As with Constable's pictures – which some researchers felt showed nothing stranger than aircraft landing lights, stars and planets – down to earth claims for the anomalies abounded. At least, they did amongst those UFO enthusiasts who didn't want to see their cherished extraterrestrial theories questioned.

There is another theory for what both Trevor James Constable and Richard Toronto photographed. It's a truly fascinating one, which was postulated by the late UFO- and paranormal-investigator, D. Scott Rogo. It was his opinion – or, perhaps, his "strong suspicion" would be better terminology – that both men had unknowingly created the sky-monsters from the depths of their imaginations and subconscious. And their psychic abilities allowed them to project their mind-monsters externally, to the point where they had quasi-independent lives and could even be caught on camera.

Whatever the truth of the matter, today, decades after he first began formulating his undeniably alternative theory for what UFOs might be, Trevor James Constable still retains a faithful following who believe our skies are not filled with extraterrestrials, but with large, flying, amoeba-like monsters.

CHAPTER 31:

THE DJINN BECOMES A HUGE
PART OF THE MOTHMAN STORY

A few years ago, I spent quite a lot of time focusing on the phenomenon of the Djinn. And, much of that same work was done with the help of the late Rosemary Ellen Guiley. The reason was because Rosemary was sure that many so-called "cryptid" creatures – such as Bigfoot, the Dog-Man, lake-monsters, the Hat-Man, Alien Big Cats, Phantom Black Dogs, and much more – were really Djinn in different forms. A fascinating theory. After all, the Djinn *is* known as an expert shapeshifter. The theory made a lot of sense. It still does. Talking of sense: I recommend that you read Rosemary's book, *The Vengeful Djinn.*

Now, to my own report on the nature of the Djinn

Of all the many and varied shapeshifters that populate our world, there is no doubt that the most feared and dreaded of all are the Djinn. They are extremely dangerous and manipulative entities that can take on various forms, and just as they see fit. It is ironic that the Djinn, in reality, is such a feared and powerful creature. The irony stems from the fact that popular culture and the world of entertainment have collectively dumbed down the nature, power, and dark characters of the Djinn. This is very much as a result of the production of the likes of the 1960s television show, *I Dream of Jeannie*, and the 1992 Disney movie, *Aladdin*. There is, however, nothing amusing or lighthearted about the real Djinn. They are the ultimate shapeshifting nightmares. And they will do all they can to get their claws into us – and particularly so if we are reckless enough to invite or invoke them.

The Djinn are entities that collectively amount to a significant part of ancient Islamic lore and teachings. Certainly, they feature prominently in the pages of the Qur'an. Muslim legend maintains that Djinns are formed out of a form of smokeless fire. Djinn expert, Rosemary Ellen Guiley has suggested that this may have been an ancient, early way of describing what, today, we would term plasma. Jesse Emspak, writing at **LiveScience**, says of plasma that it, "is a state of matter that is often thought of as a subset of gases, but the two states behave very differently. Like gases, plasmas have no fixed shape or volume, and are less dense than solids or liquids. But unlike ordinary gases, plasmas are made up of atoms in which some or all of the electrons have been stripped away and positively charged nuclei, called ions, roam freely."

The Djinn are said to be lifeforms that came into being long before the Human Race was anywhere near on the horizon. In terms of their standing – as well as their supernatural nature - in ancient religious teachings the Djinn are on a par with the angels. Again according to the old texts, after Allah brought Adam into being, each and every angel was ordered to kneel before him. While they did exactly as they were ordered, the Djinn did not. They were the ultimate rebels. The Djinn overlord, Iblis, went against Allah – as did the rest of the Djinns. The result, for them, was catastrophic: they were unceremoniously ejected from Heaven, but given the right to rectify things when Judgment Day comes calling on us all – at least, according to the ancient stories.

Of course, the story of Iblis, his rebellious followers, and their ejection from a heavenly realm closely parallels the Holy Bible's story of the Devil and deadly demons and their very own hellish domain. Might demons and Djinn be one and the very same, but given somewhat different descriptions, and histories, according to the teachings of various religions? Yes, very possibly.

Rosemary suspected that the Djinn exist in what we might call another dimension, a realm which is as unseen to us as it is impenetrable to us. But, for the Djinn, negotiating multi-dimensions is second nature – which is specifically why they spend so much time causing havoc and horror in our reality.

Unlike us, the Djinn have lifespans of such an incredible length that, compared to our measly eighty or ninety years, are akin to being almost literally immortal. They do, however, eventually die. In somewhat baffling fashion, given that they are said to be made out of plasma, Djinns have the ability to reproduce; they have families, hierarchies, and are of both sexes. They have homes, too. Their homes are far removed from ours, however.

The typical Djinn traditionally prefers Middle Eastern-based hot deserts, caverns, ancient and ruined buildings, shadowy valleys, and deep tunnels. They are not particularly enamored by daylight, much preferring instead to rest when the Sun is at its height, and to surface when the landscape is dark and filled with shadows. This, in all likelihood, explains why so many people who report Djinn encounters state that the experiences occurred after sunset and in the early hours of the morning, and specifically and usually between 1:30 a.m. and 3:00 a.m. – which parallels the malevolent activities of Incubus and Succubus. Djinn are also said to be great lovers of music – of all kinds, but particularly that played on a sitar.

Exactly how many Djinn exist – or have ever existed - is unknown; however, their extensive lifespans, combined with their abilities to procreate, suggests that they are many in number. Perhaps even millions, which is an extremely disturbing thought. This provokes an important question: if Djinn are regularly entering our world from their own dimension, then why do we not see them? According to the old tales, there is a very good answer to that question: the Djinn are invisible to the human eye. Interestingly, however, those same old tales maintain that both donkeys and dogs have the ability to see Djinn and are able to pick up on their nature, which can range from good to dangerous. In that sense, if you have a pet dog that regularly stares intently at one particular part of your living-room, and he or she reacts by shaking and whimpering, then you may have a Djinn in your very midst. Not a pleasing thought, not in the slightest. In a somewhat paradoxical state, however, the Djinn are said to keep dogs as pets – in much the same way that we do.

So, why, precisely, are the Djinn so tied to us, the Human Race? Rosemary offered the following, which is undeniably worrying: "They can eat human food when they take human form, but our food does not sustain them. It gives them pleasure. They can absorb the essence of food, and things like the molecules from tobacco smoke, which provide enjoyment. Their main source of nourishment is the absorption of energy from life forms. The best is the draining of a soul but is difficult to do and is considered unlawful. It is, however, practiced by certain powerful renegade Djinn. The vampiric absorption of the life force can be quite detrimental to people, and cause health problems."

There you have it: for the Djinn we are a source of food. But that is not all. The Djinn clearly enjoy taunting and tormenting us, too. Sometimes, this can be to a mild degree, and even relatively innocuous in nature, with Djinn moving items in the home of their target, and placing them in other rooms. This is an issue that mirrors the odd antics of so-called Tricksters like elementals, who enjoy manipulating us – chiefly for their own warped amusement. More often than not, however, the Djinn display highly dangerous activity. That very often begins with disrupting electrical equipment – everything from microwaves to refrigerators, computers to telephones, and electric lights to ovens.

Sometimes a Djinn will perform a favor for its target – which is specifically where the concept of the "Genie" and the "three wishes" derived its origins. But, it is almost always a favor that backfires, leaving the person in a far worse state than before the Djinn ever manifested. Far more disturbing: the Djinn can cause a person to fall sick – and typically dangerously so – and even to die. Paranormal infection is very often the name of their grim game.

Perhaps most malevolent of all is the ability of the Djinn to possess the mind of a person. Again, we see a parallel with biblical teachings, namely matters relative to the issue of demonic possession. This matter of the Djinn effectively taking control of, and enslaving, the mind of a specific person most often occurs when that very same person summons up a Djinn. What this demonstrates is that not only can we call forth Djinn – providing, of course, that we know the correct ancient rites that are required to do so – but that when we do so we can then become their very next victim.

As for the shapeshifting qualities of the Djinn, they are as many as they are varied. Rather notably, our old friend, the glowing-eyed Phantom Black Dog, is one of the most favored forms a Djinn will appear as, and par- ticularly so when it wishes to operate in our world. As is a snake. Indeed, according to Islamic lore, if a snake enters one's home, it may not be a normal, regular snake. In all likelihood, the old lore states, it is a shapeshifted Djinn.

Rosemary believed, and stated in her book, *The Vengeful Djinn*, that the Djinn manifest in numerous other forms, too. The long list includes aliens, the spirits of once-living people, fairies, creatures that fall into the cryptozoological domain and even angels. So clever, manipulative and cunning is the Djinn, it is incredibly difficult to determine which of the above is real and which is nothing more than a Djinn in disguise.

CHAPTER 32:

ORGONE ENERGY

Now, let's have a look at what we've found. Because of Rosemary Ellen Guiley's sterling work, we can say with some high degree of certainty that Mothman is a rogue Djinn tormenting portions of the Human Race; possibly just because…*he can*. For example, it's very easy for the Djinn to manipulate our minds. Spartanite say of the Djinn and mind-manipulation: "*When they control a human being from far, or possess them outright, all your thoughts are theirs* [italics mine]."

As for sex, which plays in with the "Lovers' Lane" enigma, *Vice* say: "According to El-Zein, the ability or desire to have sex isn't all jinn have in common with humans. Like us, jinn eat, drink, sleep, procreate and die, she says, though their mortal lives can extend for thousands of years. And yet, while we can relate to the spirits on many levels, the consensus remains that we cannot fully comprehend jinn - though we can try."

And, we should not dismiss the matter of the aforementioned shapeshifting. The Djinn can turn into multiple entities. Put all of those components together - sex energy, mind-control, the changing of ones' body – and the Djinn remains an undeniably fierce figure. Now, how about a deeper look at the way life-forces and sex work? This brings us to a man named Wilhelm Reich.

SEXUAL ENERGY: THAT'S WHY MONSTERS LIKE MOTHMAN PROWL AROUND THE WORLD'S LOVERS' LANES. INCLUDING THE ONE THAT SURFACED AT POINT PLEASANT.

As far back as the 1930s, Reich had researched what he ultimately came to call Orgone. Orgone energy. In a 2013 article titled "Understanding the Life Force Energy That Charges All of Us: Orgone Energy & the Orgone Accumulator," Mark Denicola wrote: "Orgone energy, a term coined by Reich himself, is best described as a life force energy that can be found everywhere, even on the surface of the earth. This energy, Reich believed, was capable of healing the sick, optimizing body function and even adjusting weather formation."

An important question is, of course: how did Reich reach this particular conclusion? The answer is both simple and controversial. Reich used both male and female volunteers to monitor their levels of electricity when their genitals were stimulated. By comparing those volunteers with people in non-aroused states, Reich noted something amazing: that not just sex itself, but sexual arousal and fantasizing led to profound increases in energy levels. Or, as Reich, himself, worded it, "a bio-electrical discharge," which he concluded was present in all living organisms. It became famously known as Orgone, which was derived directly from the word "orgasm."

Dr. Paul Chambers, in his 1999 book *Sex & the Paranormal*, stated: "Sexual arousal, said Reich, was like a thunderstorm, with the orgasm being like a lightning strike, discharging all the built-up sexual energy from the body."

There was far more to Reich's work, too. As well as digging deep into the mysteries of Orgone, Reich also started focusing on yet another energy-based phenomenon. He called them "Bions." They were, Reich concluded, infinitely small sacs of energy that could morph into one-celled entities. Reich said there were two kinds of Bions: the "reds" and the "blues." Incredibly, Reich claimed to be able to see the two groups of Bions essentially "fighting" each other, when placed under a microscope. This was yet another breakthrough for Reich, one which he came to believe further bolstered his belief that energy was poorly understood in the extreme – and Reich saw himself as the man who was going to find the truth.

In my own words…

Reich went on to assemble what he called an Orgone Energy Field Matter. He claimed it could measure Orgone levels in a person – and that he was able to determine the huge fluctuations between someone in a relaxed state and someone else in a highly sexual state. Next on the list was the unveiling of Reich's Orgone-Energy Accumulator. It can best be described as a large, wooden box, in which his volunteers sat. The outside of the Orgone-Energy Accumulator would be coated with organic materials; the interior, however, was made of metal. Reich believed that Orgone would be attracted to the external side, and would then radiate within the box, thus bathing the person in Orgone and, thereby, increasing their energy levels. The more and more he dug into his Orgone-based research, the more and more Reich came to believe that Orgone had the potential ability to cure some of the most serious conditions on the planet – including cancer – as well as psychological conditions, such as sexual anxieties, neuroses and much more. Reich's work attracted the attention of numerous famous people in the field of the arts, including Jack Kerouac, William S. Burroughs, and J.D. Salinger.

That Reich concluded Orgone had an attraction to, and an affinity for, water, led him to believe he could use targeted Orgone to manipulate the weather, too. In other words, complete weather-control. Powerful winds, storms, deluges, and thunder and lightning: Reich saw himself as the man who could just about command them all. It was not destined to be, however.

Although the U.S. Food and Drug Administration (FDA) took a decidedly dim view of Reich's work and his alternative theories, he certainly had a massive following – all of whom felt that the sexual energy known as Orgone was, essentially, the equivalent of a huge, powerful battery that could both energize and revitalize. Throughout the late-1940s and into the early-to-mid-1950s, Reich was someone who many listened to – and who listened very carefully. Between 1948 and up until the time of his death, just a little less than a decade later, Reich wrote many successful books, including, *Ether, God, and Devil*; *Cosmic Superimposition*; *The Invasion of Compulsory Sex-Morality*; and *People in Trouble*.

Eventually, for the FDA enough was most definitely enough. Reich's real troubles began in February 1954, when the United States Attorney for the District of Maine sought an injunction to prevent Reich from selling his accumulators outside of his home-state. It worked; although Reich could not have cared less. He continued to sell them, and the government be damned. Then, in May 1956, Reich found himself in majorly hot water when an employee of the FDA posed as someone wanting an accumulator of their very own...and who conveniently wanted it shipped out of state. Reich was delighted to oblige – until, that is, the truth behind the FDA's ruse hit him squarely in the face. He was, in essence, busted. Most disturbing of all, a number of Reich's books were quickly withdrawn from availability by the government. And, shortly afterwards, hundreds of copies of his titled were not just confiscated, but *burned*. To say that it was a definitive witch-hunt would not be far off the mark.

One month later, the FDA descended on Reich's labs and ordered that his accumulators be destroyed. There was very little that Reich could do to prevent such a thing from happening. Then, in August 1956, no less than *six tons* of Reich's materials – his journals, the remaining copies of his books, and his mass of equipment and more - were ordered to be destroyed, in what turned out to be a blazing inferno. Following that, there was the not insignificant matter of a two-year prison term for what was perceived by the U.S. Government as Reich having sold bogus technologies. Reich didn't last long, though: he was found dead, on November 3, 1957, in the Lewisburg Federal Penitentiary, Pennsylvania. The verdict was heart failure. He was just sixty.

There are indications that even today the government has its uneasy concerns about Reich and his work. In

1999 the FBI placed into the public domain almost eight hundred pages of previously-classified files on Reich. The documents were soon uploaded to the FBI's website. Eight years later, however, the documents were quietly removed. The file continues to remain absent from its original website – as well as from the FBI's additional site, "The Vault," which was created in 2011. The FBI states that the file was removed as it was not seen as being historically valuable. Reich's followers would certainly disagree with that conclusion. Fortunately, the FBI's file on Reich can still be found online – at archive.org – under the title of "Wilhelm Reich: Federal Bureau of Investigation."

As for Reich's almost legendary Orgone, even though U.S. authorities had no time for it and did all they could to shut Reich's work down – and succeeded in doing so – it's an important part of the story of paranormal parasites in our midst. In fact, it's a vital component of the overall controversy. As we have seen, Reich concluded that Orgone was a form of sexual energy that acted – in near-identical fashion – as a battery. Orgone could be directed into a person and offer them a new life, one filled with vigor and absent of anxieties. More importantly, though, Orgone could be *removed* from the body: it is basically the equivalent of putting the accumulator in reverse.

And, now, we know that while Reich was studying Orgone, Mothman was using it as a form of "fuel" for the human body. Hence the reason as to why there are so many Lovers' Lanes in the world. That's yet *another* reason to believe that the Mothman is a Djinn.

CONCLUSIONS

There's no doubt that the "flying humanoid" phenomenon is a real one. It might have been here, on Earth, for centuries. Millennia, possibly." *Maybe, forever.* Who can say for sure? As we've seen, their names include Mothman, the Vietnam winged woman, the Houston Batman, the Batsquatch, the Owlman, the Yorkshire Pterodactyl and numerous more. Not only that, those creatures of the skies are tied to disaster and death – and not just to Point Pleasant.

Monster-seeker Jonathan Downes had to leave – and *quickly* leave - his interest in the matter of the Owlman of England for the sake of his health and his life. And, John *did* stay away, such were his fears of those sky-creatures. Remember that: these monsters are experts when it comes to paranormal backlash, as Jon called it. And, they won't fail to use it when they need it.

There's also the matter of these entities being able to alter their forms, as we've seen. We're talking about creatures that can morph their forms. For example, the good folk of Point Pleasant have seen giant-sized, bird-like animals over their homes. Others have encountered bat-type things. Then, there are those who - over Point Pleasant - suggest these creatures are Native American Thunderbirds. Think of the Houston Batman that was seen back in the 1950s: that was a definitive humanoid with wings. But, nothing like a Thunderbird. The creatures might look somewhat different, but the wings are always there. As are those red eyes. They will always be here. Everywhere.

As for those prophecies – in both the 1960s and years later, as we've seen – they came to be absolutely real. With that on our minds, here's a good question: how do we define a prophecy? Cambridge Dictionary present it perfectly: "A statement that says what is going to happen in the future, especially one that is based on what you believe about a particular matter rather than existing facts."

Medium.com have a perfect description, too: "Prophetic dreams are dreams where you have an experience that has yet to happen in our realm of existence *but later happens* [italics mine], where you will experience Deja vu from already having seen the result of that experience."

And, we know that such happenings are relative to the Mothman controversy, too. In fact, this was what happened when the Silver Bridge collapsed at the Ohio River. As the website *Chasing the Frog* state: "A dream prophecy was reported and the event happened; however, it was not the same premonition as in the [2002] movie. Mary Hyre, a newspaper reporter that often accompanied Mr. Keel in Point Pleasant investigations, dreamt that there were a lot of people drowning in the river and Christmas packages were floating everywhere in the water."

So, yes, prophecies are realities. But, sometimes, what should be clear seems to be murky.

Then, there's the matter of those latter-day prophecies; those that swamped Chicago with nightmares in 2017/2018, when Mothman was gliding the skies at night. This is where matters get complicated: some of the key prophecies have proved to be accurate. On other occasions, however, accuracy was nowhere near in sight. It was very much the same with those terrifying, nuclear dreams so many people were exposed to in the dead of night. Not only that, it almost sounds like the poor victims of those nightmares were *deliberately* – and *evilly* – "played" with by Mothman. Manipulated? But, why? Why *this* person? Why *that* person? To suck in our sexual energy - Orgone – just like we would fill our cars with gas? A viable theory.

Quite possibly, the only answer to all of this is the one that can be found in the fictional 2002 movie, *The Mothman Prophecies*. In the movie, actor Alan Bates – playing character "Alexander Leek" – says, in a slightly weird fashion, that when it comes to investigating Mothman, supernatural entities and other paranormal activity, "*We're not allowed to know.*"

BIBLIOGRAPHY

Barker, Gray. *Bender Mystery Confirmed.*
Saucerian Books. 1962.

Barker, Gray. *The Silver Bridge.* Saucerian Books. 1970.

Blood Beast Terror, The. https://www.
imdb.com/title/tt0061411/. 2023.

Britannica. *Jinni: Arabian mythology.* https://
www.britannica.com/topic/jinni. 2023.

Cambridge Dictionary. "Prophecy." https://
dictionary.cambridge.org/us/dictionary/
english/prophecy?q=prophecies. 2023.

Chambers, Paul. Dr. *Sex & the Paranormal.* Blandford. 1999.

Cold, Indrid. https://en.wikipedia.org/wiki/
Indrid_Cold. 2023. January 10,

Coleman, Loren. Cryptozoonews. *Soldier of Fortune:
Mothman Sightings Were Merely Green Beret.* http://
www.cryptozoonews.com/sof-mm/. 2014.

Coleman, Loren. *Mothman: Evil
Incarnate.* Cosimo Books. 2017.

Collins, Andrew. *The Brentford Griffin: The Truth
Behind the Tales.* Earthquest Books. 1985.

Constable, Trevor James. *They Live in the Sky.* Book Tree. 2016.

Davies, Ross, BBC. *Threads.* https://www.bbc.
com/culture/article/20190925-was-threads-
the-scariest-tv-show-ever-made. 1984.

Derenberger, Woody. https://www.encyclope-dia.com/science/encyclopedias-almanacs- tran-scripts-and-maps/derenberger-woodrow. 2023.

Dictionary.com. *Zeitgeist*. https://www.dic-tionary.com/browse/zeitgeist. 2023.

Division of Environmental Health Office of Radiation Protection. Electromagnetic Pulse (EMP). https://doh.wa.gov/sites/default/files/legacy/Documents/Pubs/320-090_elecpuls_fs.pdf. September 2003.

Downes, Jonathan. The Center for Fortean Zoology. https://cfz.org.uk/. 2023.

Downes, Jonathan. *The Owlman and Others*. CFZ Press. 2006.

Ettachfini, Leila. What are Jinn: The Arab Spirits Who Can Eat, Sleep, Have Sex and Die. https://www.vice.com/en/arti-cle/9k7ekv/what-are jinn-arab-spirits. October 31, 2018.

Forteana.org. *Pennine Pterodactyl*. https://obscurban- leg-end.fandom.com/wiki/Pennine_Pterodactyl. 2023.

Gerhard, Ken. *Encounters with Flying Humanoids*. Llewellyn Publications. 2013.

Griffin, Andrew W. "Riders on the storm (Strange days have tracked us down)." http://www.red-dirtreport.com/red-dirt-grit/riders-storm-strange-days-have-tracked-us-down. August 15, 2017.

Haunted Librarian, The. *Mothman was a…Green Beret?* https://thehauntedlibrarian.com/2017/02/17/mothman-was-a-green-beret/. Feb 17, 2017.

John and Tim Frick. https://themothman.fan-dom.com/wiki/John_And_Tim_Frick. 2023.

Johnkeel.com. *Mothman in Soldier of Fortune.*
https://www.johnkeel.com/?p=2138.

Jornlin, Allison. *American Ghost Walks.* 2023. https://
www.americanghostwalks.com/articles/aj-at-paramooc.

Keel, John A. The *Mothman Prophecies.* IllumiNet Press. 1991.

Making Britain. *George Edalji.* January 9, 2014.
https://www.open.ac.uk/researchprojects/mak-
ingbritain/content/george-edalji. 2023.

Lowth, Marcus. *The Dark Forces at Work Over the United
Kingdom in 1963?* https://www.ufoinsight.com/supernatural/
time/dark-forces-united-kingdom-1963. June 27, 2020.

McNabb, Max. *The Legendary Sighting of the Houston
Batman: A Flying Monster?* https://texashillcountry.com/
houston-batman-flying-monster/. September 30, 2018.

Medium.com. The 4 Types Of Dreams, And How To Start
Having More Prophetic Dreams Nightly. June 28, 2019. https://
medium.com/holisticism/the-4-types-of-dreams-and-how-to-
start-having-more- prophetic-dreams-nightly-53260e47cc9d.

Medway, Gareth. *Men in Black Encounters, a Short Catalog.*
https://pelicanist.blogspot.com/p/mib-encounters.html. 2023.

Morgawr. https://cryptidz.fandom.com/wiki/Morgawr. 2023.

Mothman Wikia, The. *Chief Cornstalk.* https://themoth-
man.fandom.com/wiki/Chief_Cornstalk. 2023.

Music Box Theater. *Q: The Winged Serpent.* https://music-
boxtheatre.com/films-and-events/q-the-winged-serpent. 2023.

Obscurban Legends. *Glowing Winged Woman of
Vietnam.* https://obscurban- legend.fandom.com/
wiki/Glowing_Winged_Woman_of_Vietnam

O'Neill, Claire. *Welcome to the 'TNT Area' Home of the Mothman.* 2023. https://www.npr.org/sections/picture-show/2012/01/23/145334460/welcome-to-the-tnt-area-home-of-the-mothman. January 23, 2012.

PSI Encyclopedia. *Thoughtforms.* https://psi-encyclopedia.spr.ac.uk/articles/thoughtforms. 2023.

Randall, Elizabeth. *Tales of the Mysterious and Curious.* Kithra. September 8, 2017.

Redfern, Nick. *Chupacabra Road Trip.* Llewellyn Publications. 2015.

Redfern, Nick. *The Monster Book: Creatures, Beasts and Fiends of Nature.* Visible Ink Press. 2017.

Sheppard, Susan. *The Gallows Tree: A Mothman's Tale.* PublishAmerica. November 23, 2004.

Spartanite. How Djinn (Jinn) Use Telepathy For complete Mind Control. https://www.thespartanite.com/2023/02/27/how-djinn-jinn-use-telepathy-for-complete-mind- control/. February 27, 2023.

Steiger, Brad. *Psychic City Chicago.* Doubleday & Company, Inc. 1976.

Strickler, Lon. *Mothman Dynasty: Chicago's Winged Humanoids.* Triangulum Publishing. 2017.

Strieber, Whitley. *The Secret School: Preparation for Contact.* Harper Collins. 1997.

Strieber, Whitley. *Warday.* Warner Books. 1984.

SyFy. *Proof Positive.* https://en.wikipedia.org/wiki/Proof_Positive_(TV_series). 2004.

U.S. Nuclear Regulatory Commission. *Backgrounder on Chernobyl Nuclear Power Plant Accident.* https://www.nrc.gov/reading-rm/doc-collections/fact-sheets/chernobyl-bg.html. March 1, 2022.

Villains Wiki. *Kongamato.* https://villains.fan-dom.com/wiki/Kongamato. 2023.

Wamsley, Jeff. *Mothman: Behind the Red Eyes.* Mothman Press. 2020.

Wayland, Tobias. *The Lake Michigan Mothman: High Strangeness in the Midwest.* Singular Fortean Publishing. 2019.

Weatherly, David. *Black Eyed Children.* 2nd Edition. Erie Lights Publishing. 2022.

Acknowledgements

Many thanks to my agent and publisher
Lisa Hagan and Simon Hartshorne who created
the great cover of the book and the layout, too.

Made in the USA
Coppell, TX
02 June 2024